**CONTRIBUTIONS
OF WOMEN**

DANCE

by Carol Fowler

Dillon Press, Inc.
Minneapolis, Minnesota

Dillon Press, Inc., 500 South Third Street
Minneapolis, Minnesota 55415

Printed in the United States of America

Library of Congress Cataloging in Publication Data

Fowler, Carol.
  Dance.

  (Contributions of women)
  Bibliography: p. 127
  SUMMARY: Brief biographies of five women who have
made important contributions to the field of dance, Isadora
Duncan, Martha Graham, Agnes de Mille, Twyla Tharp, and
Gelsey Kirkland. Includes information about 10 other out-
standing female dancers.
  women 1. Dancers—Biography—Juvenile literature.
  [1. Dancers]   I. Title.
  GV1785.A1F66   793.3'2'0922 [B] [920]   78-10313
  ISBN 0-87518-169-4

Contents

Photographs reproduced through the courtesy of the American Ballet Theatre, Aaron Copland, the Music and Performing Arts Department of the Detroit Public Library, the Martha Graham Center of Contemporary Dance, Inc., the Martha Graham Dance Company, the New York City Ballet, the Dance Collection of the New York Public Library at Lincoln Center, the North Carolina School of the Arts, the Twyla Tharp Dance Foundation, Inc., and the Wisconsin Center for Film and Theatre Research.

Introduction

"Dancing is too hard a life to consider lightly," Martha Graham has told young people who have come to her, asking to be her students. "Dancing is a call. You either *have* to be a dancer or you don't. Free choice doesn't enter into it."

All of the dancers whose stories are told in the following pages were "called" in the way that Graham uses the word. Their desire to dance was so great that it overshadowed everything else in their lives, and it gave them a belief in themselves that led to greatness.

Isadora Duncan was praised for daring in the concert halls of Europe at a time when the United States was little respected for its contributions to the arts. Martha Graham's genius gave life to an entirely new way of moving and sharing feelings. Agnes de Mille brought the best of dance and theater together. Today, Twyla Tharp is using the ideas and music of our time in her bold, brilliant dance while young Gelsey Kirkland brings her grace to the time-honored beauty of classic ballet.

Their efforts and the efforts of countless others, some of whom are described briefly in the last section of this book, have made dance in America today an exciting calling. Dance companies have grown both in importance and numbers. Audiences have increased by fifteen times in the last ten years. At the center of this excitement are the women of dance—the stars, the dancers of the company, and the choreographers.

DANCING
REBEL

ISADORA DUNCAN: She dreamed of the Dance of the Future.

In 1895 many seventeen-year-old girls were still in school or leading a quiet life at home. For the most part, only those who had to help support their families worked. They had jobs—as servants, storeclerks, and factory workers—rather than careers. But seventeen-year-old Isadora Duncan had no taste for security. Even though she was the youngest of four children, she acted as head of the family.

One warm summer day Isadora gathered her family about her and told them that she was leaving San Francisco. If she was going to get anywhere in her career as a dancer, she had to go east. She and her mother would leave right away. After she had earned enough money, she would send for her sister Elizabeth and her two brothers, Raymond and Augustin.

Isadora and her mother traveled to Chicago in two tourist seats on the train. The damp heat of the Midwest beat down on them as they walked from theater to theater, looking for work. But as soon as she began to dance, Isadora forgot her weariness. The music she chose for her auditions was Mendelssohn's "Spring Song," and the dance was her very own.

It was a lovely dance and so was her costume—a simple white tunic. But the theater managers shook their heads. The dance was for the church, they said, not for the theater. The twenty-five dollars the Duncans had brought dwindled away. They sold a few antique pins and finally, Isadora had to sell the lace collar from her dress. Then she auditioned for Charles Fair, the manager of the Masonic Roof Garden. He did not refuse as quickly as the others, but he told her that her graceful dance would not do. He wanted something with pep in it, and he would like to see frills on her costume.

Isadora agreed. The time had come when she had to find some kind of work. She bought some red material and white ruffles on credit, and her mother made her a pretty ruffled skirt. When Isadora auditioned again for the manager of the roof garden, she wore her new red skirt and danced to a snappy marching tune. This time she pleased him, and he hired her as "The California Faun."

Isadora, however, was not pleased. The fast dance in the gaudy costume went against her ideas of what dance was meant to be. She quit the job after three weeks even though Fair wanted her to stay on. According to her autobiography, *My Life,* Isadora never again performed for an audience in a way that went against her ideals. Young as she was, Isadora knew what those ideals were. When she pressed Augustin Daly, a well-known theater manager of the day, into giving her an audition, she gave him a lecture, too!

"I have discovered the dance," Isadora said grandly. "For the children of America I will create a new dance that will express America." And Isadora Duncan did go on to create "a new dance." Her idea that dance should express thoughts and feelings rather than follow the studied movements of classical ballet was to bring great changes to the world of dance.

She was born in San Francisco on May 27, 1878, to Mary Dora Duncan. Isadora's father, Joseph Charles Duncan, had left his family before her birth, and her parents were soon divorced.

Isadora saw her father only a few times in her life. He was a mysterious person whose name was never mentioned, and Isadora found no one in her family willing to explain the meaning of her parents' marriage and divorce to her. When she was all of twelve years old, Isadora decided that marriage was unjust to women. She would "fight against marriage," as she wrote in *My Life,* "and for the right of every woman to have a child or children as it pleased her, and to uphold her right and her virtue."

Isadora never liked school. In part, she felt the embarrassment of being a poor child. Her shoes often had holes, and her stomach rumbled from being empty. Most of all, she hated the conformity that was expected of her. Facts had to be memorized; students had to sit on hard benches all day. Her real education came at home when her mother read poetry or played Beethoven, Mozart, and Chopin on the piano.

Some of her earliest dancing lessons were given to toddlers in the neighborhood. She plopped the children on the floor and taught them to move their arms like the ocean waves. When she was fourteen, she held regular dance classes. By then, she had persuaded her mother to allow her to quit school. When she was fifteen, Isadora's father provided a house for the family on Van Ness Street in San Francisco. It was an old mansion with large rooms that were splendid for dance classes, and there was a carriage house in the back. Isadora's brother Augustin made the carriage house into a theater where the four Duncans gave plays and shows. It was about this time that Isadora decided to improve her chances for a dance career by going to Chicago.

Although Augustin Daly, the man she lectured on American dance, did not take her up on her idea, he did give her a small part in *Miss Pygmalion.* Isadora was so sure she was on her way to success that she borrowed a hundred dollars from a friend and brought her family to New York City, where *Miss Pygmalion* was performed in the fall of 1895. The following year she joined Daly's Shakespearean repertory company, dancing in *A Midsummer Night's Dream.*

Meanwhile, the Duncans moved from boardinghouse to boardinghouse in New York City until they were able to rent a large studio in Carnegie Hall. Isadora left the Daly company to devote all her time to inventing new movements and steps for her dances. She worked them out carefully so that each time she repeated a dance, her movements were the same. She was developing a method that she could teach to the students who came to the studio.

Society women flocked to her recitals. They loved the graceful dances that Isadora invented, and they asked her to dance at their parties. Occasionally someone in the audience was shocked by Isadora's short tunic and bare legs. At this time female dancers, like other women, were well covered up when they performed. Isadora herself was not happy about dancing at these parties. She sensed that her wealthy patrons liked her as a kind of pet, and she longed to find a place where her ideals of dancing would be truly appreciated. She thought again of moving farther east—this time to Europe. In the early summer of 1899, the Duncans boarded a cattle boat and sailed for London.

When they arrived in England, Isadora took letters of introduction from her New York patrons to the society hostesses of London. Once more she was performing in the homes of the rich. At one of these performances she met Charles Hallé, a painter and the son of a famous conductor.

Hallé and his friends introduced Isadora to Greek art, drama, and philosophy. She spent hours with them in the British Museum as she studied the ancient marble statues from the Parthenon and the dancing figures on Greek vases and urns. She began to work the poses of these figures into her own dances. Sometimes Isadora spoke of her dance as a series of poses. As one position melted in natural, graceful movement, it created the next, and then the next. She became known as the Greek dancer. People had the mistaken idea that she wanted to revive the ancient Greek style of dancing. This was not the case. Isadora wanted to achieve in her dance the ideals of beauty that she had found in the art of the ancient Greeks.

Isadora worked very hard—refining old techniques and inventing new ideas. She started to dance barefoot on a carpet, since it added naturalness to her movements. Wanting to discover the point in her body where her movements originated, she stood still for long periods, her hands clasped over her chest. She came to understand that at a point deep in her chest there existed a central spring, or source, of movement. Isadora listened intently to the music—with her soul—she said. Then she moved her body, arms, and legs from this point in her chest. Because ballet movements originate at the base of the spine rather than from the natural center of the chest, she thought they gave the dancer a puppet-like appearance. Isadora was gradually developing a theory of dance.

In late 1901, Loie Fuller, a well-known American dancer, visited her in Paris, where Isadora now lived with her mother and Raymond. Fuller saw something new and exciting in the young dancer's work, and she asked Isadora to join a tour she had planned. Instead of the homes of the rich, Isadora now danced in enormous theaters. In Vienna, a theatrical manager, Alexander Gross, lured Isadora away from Loie Fuller and booked her in solo recitals for Budapest, Munich, and Berlin. This tour was the start of Isadora's world-wide reputation. She danced her way to fame across Europe.

At that time, audiences were used to lavish productions that had many dancers, fancy costumes, and dazzling stage scenery. Isadora danced a program of eight or ten numbers all by herself. Barefooted, she wore only a tunic. A belt or a ribbon was all that was needed to make it look like a Grecian dress or a gown of the Italian Renaissance. She used curtains as a backdrop instead of stage scenery. But her emotional appeal to the audience was so great that they sat spellbound. By the time she danced in Berlin in 1903, her fame was so great that when she left the theater, students unhitched the horses from her carriage and pulled it through the streets to her hotel.

Isadora had earned a great deal of money from these solo recitals—enough to take her entire family to Greece in late 1903. Wearing the dress of the ancient Greeks and sandals, she startled the citizens of Athens as she walked the streets where her ideals had been born. She prowled ruins and museums; she visited the sites of legend—Delphi and Leucadi; and she danced in the ancient, deserted Theater of Dionysus.

Here, where ancient Greek dance and drama had begun, was the place that Isadora belonged. Her family felt so too, for they shared her ideals of art as well as her life. They bought a parcel of land near the Parthenon upon which they would build a temple of their own. They insisted that it had to be built in the ancient Greek way. Isadora laid the cornerstone according to the old rituals and danced the old dances with her brother Raymond. The walls of their temple would be two feet thick, just like those of the ancient Palace of Agamemnon. Little donkeys worked hard as they hauled huge, heavy red stones to the hilltop site. The Duncans were well into the project when they discovered that there was no way to install water in their temple, unless one wanted to bring it up the hill in buckets! They had paid a lot of money for land that was worthless to them.

It did not take long for Isadora's funds to run out. Late one night she went to the Parthenon by herself and reached a painful decision. "Suddenly," she wrote in *My Life,* "it seemed to me as if all our dreams burst like a glorious bubble, and we were not, nor ever could be, other than moderns. We could not have the feeling of the Ancient Greeks. . . . I was, after all, but a Scotch-Irish-American." It was time to give up their dreams. Three days later they left Greece, and Isadora began another European tour.

Isadora, dressed like the Greeks of long ago.

During these creative years, from her early to her mid-twenties, Isadora not only put new movements and gestures into her dances, but she also wrote down her ideas and delivered a lecture on the subject. In 1904, her lecture, "The Dance of the Future," was published in Germany. Her ideas about natural, graceful movements were discussed and influenced the thinking of people involved in dance. Then a week-long series of performances in Saint Petersburg, Russia, in 1904, probably brought about more changes in ballet than her written words or any earlier performances.

Saint Petersburg was the ballet capital of the world in 1904. The Russian Imperial Ballet, supported by the czars, the rulers of Russia, was the home of the greatest dancers and choreographers of that time. Two of them, Michel Fokine and Sergei Diaghilev, came to Isadora's first performance in Saint Petersburg. Nearly everything she did was new to them: her use of classical music, her comfortable tunics, and her flowing movements. In ballet, music was written expressly for the stories "told" in the dance. The dancer wore toe shoes, tights, and billowing skirts, and the movements were based on formal positions.

Michel Fokine was so impressed that he made Isadora's ideas part of the ballets he created. Today, almost any program of classic ballet includes Fokine's ballets set to the music of Chopin. In this way, the formal dance of ballet incorporated Isadora's "Dance of the Future."

In 1905, Isadora made one of her dreams for the dance come true. She purchased a house in a suburb of Berlin, which she made into a school. The "new dance for children" that she so boldly described when she was seventeen was about to take life.

She transformed the drab villa she had bought.

The walls were painted blue and white. Reproductions of famous Greek statues and paintings with classic themes decorated the rooms. The blue and white canopied beds Isadora chose were a special treat for the poor little girls who lived at the school. They wore short, simple tunics like Isadora's long one, and they had plenty of fresh air and exercise.

In the ten years since Isadora set out for Chicago to seek fame and fortune, she had found both. And she had seen her dreams become reality in the school. Then her personal life reached a high point as well. She met Gordon Craig, a British theatrical designer, at her home in December 1904. They fell deeply in love, but neither Craig nor Isadora felt that they should marry. In 1906 Isadora was delighted to discover that she was going to have a baby.

At that time it took great courage to go against one of the important values of society—that a mother be a married woman. Amidst a storm of protest by some of the wealthy patrons of her school, Isadora went quietly to a villa on the North Sea to await the birth of her child. On September 24, 1906, her daughter, Deirdre, was born.

When she was able to perform again, Isadora had to go on tour, for the expenses of the school kept her continually on the edge of debt. She also had total responsibility for Deirdre since Craig had left to carry on his career elsewhere and Isadora did not want to give up her own plans to follow him.

Stories of Isadora's great popularity and descriptions of her dances were printed in newspapers in Europe and the United States. The idea of the "Greek" dancing became a popular notion, and many imitators of her style appeared. None of them matched her artistry since they used only those features of her dance, such as her tunics and the Strauss waltzes, that could be easily copied. Rarely did they understand the years of study and depth of technique that had created Isadora's style.

Isadora returned to the United States for the first time in 1908, nine years after she had left her own country as an unknown dancer. Now she was famous, but she was in desperate need of money. The school in Germany had been forced to close for lack of funds, and her twelve remaining students had to be cared for.

Although she had taken Europe by storm, her performances in New York fell flat. Booked for a slack period, August, Isadora found that the audiences were slim and the reviews critical. Some Americans were bewildered by the graceful dancing to classical music and the idea of one person performing the entire program. People had also read in the newspapers about Isadora's choice to have a child while unmarried, and many disapproved of her decision. Unfortunately, their disapproval was often transferred to criticism of her dancing.

Disappointed at the cool welcome in her own country, Isadora cancelled the rest of her tour and took a studio in New York. Artists, poets, and musicians remained a small, but loyal, following, and they came to the studio to see her. One well-known conductor, Walter Damrosch, thought it was unfortunate that she would not perform any more in New York. He arranged for a program at the Metropolitan Opera House with his orchestra, the New York Symphony Orchestra.

As soon as the first movement of Beethoven's Seventh Symphony reached her ears, Isadora moved, putting meaning and grace into her gestures that reflected the great music. The audience responded, and she continued on a tour far more successful than the attempt a few months earlier. In Washington, D.C., President Theodore Roosevelt watched her dance and said that her performance was as innocent as a child dancing through the garden. She ended the tour with a considerable amount of money.

Soon Isadora performed at the Gaieté-Lyrique Théatre in Paris, where once again people scrambled for tickets, cheered, and threw flowers on the stage. Following the cheers, Isadora always stepped to the front of the stage and spoke to the audience. She explained her ideals of the dance and how she wished to inspire children with those ideals. Then she made a plea for financial support for a school.

Isadora needed the help of wealthy patrons, and she found one when she met Paris Singer, the son of the founder of the Singer sewing machine company. A rich American, he had spent most of his adult life in Europe. Singer introduced himself to Isadora after one of her performances at the Gaieté-Lyrique. Soon afterwards he offered her the use of his villa in Nice and then took Isadora and Deirdre on a trip around Italy on his yacht. Isadora was falling in love again, and so was Singer. When they returned to Paris, Isadora left him to fulfill engagements in Russia, and a second tour of the United States soon followed.

She looked forward to having Singer's child with great joy. Their son Patrick was born May 1, 1910. During the next several months Isadora enjoyed living in elegant, expensive hotels. She wore fashionable gowns made by the best designers in Paris rather than flowing Greek tunics. During the summer she took her two children to Singer's home in the English countryside. Growing bored and restless, she began to practice daily for a third American tour. Although it was fun for a while, Isadora had no intention of retiring to lead an idle, rich life.

During her 1911 American tour, she danced nearly an entire opera, Gluck's *Orpheo*. She gave a performance as demanding as any athlete's with such vitality and beauty that American audiences warmed to her at last. Parts of the program were cheered for so long that Isadora repeated them for encores.

Happy to return to France and her two children, she settled into a house that she had bought from an artist in Neuilly, near Paris. Singer wanted to build a theater for her, where her school would also be housed. He chose a site on the Champs Elysées, the fashionable boulevard in the heart of Paris. She consulted with designers and architects, who built a model of the building.

Deirdre, now seven, loved to dance with her mother, and Isadora hoped that Deirdre would carry on the school of the dance for children. She thought that her daughter was her best pupil. Little Patrick, on the other hand, had a mind of his own and would not let his mother teach him. In her autobiography she remembers him saying, "No. Patrick will dance Patrick's own dance alone."

At thirty-five, Isadora appeared to be at the peak of her creative powers, and she was deeply happy. Then tragedy struck—a tragedy that in Isadora's words "was to end all hopes of any natural, joyous life for me—for ever after."

Singer had taken Isadora, her children, and six students out to lunch. They talked excitedly about the plans for the new theater. "It will be Patrick's Theater," Isadora said, "for Patrick is the Great Composer, who will create the Music to the Dance of the Future."

Isadora with her children, Deirdre (left) and Patrick (right). Like his mother in the photo on page 14, the long-haired little boy looks as if he is posing for an ancient painting or sculpture.

After lunch, Isadora had returned to her studio when Singer burst in and cried, "The children—the children—are dead!"

On their way home, the car in which Deirdre and Patrick were riding had swerved to avoid a taxi and stalled. After the driver got out of the car, it started to roll downhill and plunged into the Seine. Deirdre and the nurse had drowned. Patrick died a short time later in the hospital.

Isadora never recovered from the blow. In a letter to the architect who had planned "Patrick's Theater," she said that she was haunted by the memory of her children waving to her as the car drove off. As for the theater, only a model remained. Isadora wandered aimlessly in Greece and Italy for nearly a year as she tried to escape the memory of Deirdre and Patrick. There were times when she felt that she would never be able to dance in public again.

Eventually her grief dulled enough for her to respond to the chance to see her old dream come true. Singer telegraphed her and said that it was now possible for her to set up her school in France. He had bought an old hotel at Bellevue, outside of Paris. Isadora returned at once and began to turn the sixty-two room building into a school for her Dance of the Future.

She believed that she would spend the rest of her life at Bellevue, but she lived her dream for only seven short months. World War I began in August 1914. The French were in desperate need of hospitals for their wounded soldiers. In a grand gesture that she later regretted, she lent Bellevue to the Red Cross to be made into a hospital. When it was returned to her after the war, the building needed so much work to restore it that it had to be sold.

Isadora did not return to her hometown of San Francisco until she toured California in 1917. She had spent the greater part of twenty-two years in Europe, and yet she considered her dance to be American. In the vast open spaces of her own country she imagined she could see Americans dance, just as the poet Walt Whitman, a great favorite of hers, wrote that he could hear Americans singing. She believed that her dance had its origins not with the ancient Greeks, but in the American spirit of her grandmother's jigs, the dances of the American Indians, and "Yankee Doodle Dandy." She was one of the first Americans, in any art form, to bring the ways of the new world to the old.

During the war and for several years afterwards, Isadora was defeated time and time again in her efforts to support herself and found a school of dance. Money was a constant problem as she toured the United States, France, and the countries in South America. Her pupils were shunted from New York to Zurich and back to New York again. Their numbers dwindled to five loyal girls, who had attended her first school in Berlin and to whom she gave her own name in 1920. They were growing up and were eager to begin careers of their own.

In the spring of 1921, Isadora's latest attempt to start a school, this time in Greece, had just come to a disappointing end. She found herself once more in Paris, once more facing an uncertain future. Then she received a telegram that seemed to promise the best plan of all. "Come to Moscow," it said. "We will give you school and thousand children. You may carry on your idea on a big scale."

Leonid Krasin, an official of the Soviet government, had seen Isadora perform in London. To Tchaikovsky's "Marche Slav," music that had been written in praise

Isadora, surrounded by her students, in 1917.

of Russia under the czars, Isadora had brought new meaning. She portrayed a captive struggling against her chains and then freeing herself in triumph. Krasin was deeply moved by a dance so symbolic of the Russian Revolution.

Russia was now firmly under the control of the Communists. Westerners had a deep distrust of the new government, and there were rumors of the people's terrible suffering. Millions of Russians had died or had fled abroad. Children were starving, rumor said, and even being eaten! Isadora's friends and pupils begged her not to go. Only Isadora and Irma Duncan, her oldest student, were in favor of the idea. "Don't worry, Irma," she said to her adopted daughter. "They'll eat me first anyway. There is a whole lot more of me than you."

The first children Isadora saw in Russia were in no danger of being eaten, but they were hungry and in rags. Her train had stopped at dawn just inside the Russian border, and curious children crowded around her. Isadora played some records for them and gave them a dancing lesson. She also handed out all of the food she had with her. When she arrived in Moscow, her food was rationed like everyone else's. She received a portion every two weeks, and towards the end of the second week she and Irma often had only potatoes left to eat.

There were housing problems, too. They had to move from borrowed apartment to borrowed apartment until they finally moved into the huge gray stone building that became the school. Gradually, pupils enrolled in the school, but not in the numbers Isadora had been promised. There were only about fifty when she gave her first recital on November 7, 1921, the fourth anniversary of the Russian Revolution. Lenin, the founder of the Russian Communist Party and Soviet Russia's first dictator, was there. He sang the "Internationale," the Communist anthem, with others in the audience as Isadora danced to it. After her performance of "Marche Slav," he rose to his feet and cried, "Bravo, bravo, Miss Duncan."

Only a few days after her successful recital, Isadora came face to face with an old problem. Government officials told her that theater performances were no longer free. Just as in any other country, tickets had to be purchased for a performance. Since Isadora would receive money for her recitals, it was no longer necessary for the government to support the school. Her school could earn enough to pay its way, they said. Isadora knew better. In the spring of 1922 she left Russia for a tour of Germany and the United States, and she took her new husband with her. Disaster after disaster followed.

Sergei Essenin was a brilliant, though unstable, Russian poet. He was fifteen years younger than Isadora and did not speak her language. Isadora broke her vows never to marry so that the Russian government would let him travel with her. She had not only fallen in love with Essenin, but she also felt that he should travel outside his own country.

During the tour, Essenin felt overshadowed by Isadora, and he was isolated from others because he spoke only Russian. He drank heavily, and when drunk, went to great lengths to draw attention to himself. The couple were thrown out of hotels, and the press made much of their scenes in public. In the United States, people were terrified that Communists would try to overthrow their own government. Isadora's interpretations of the "Marche Slav" and the "Internationale" branded her as

Isadora and her husband, Sergei Essenin, a young poet whom she met in Russia.

a dangerous revolutionary. After the mayor told her to leave Boston, her performances were canceled in city after city. When she finished what was left of her tour, she told newspaper reporters that she would never come back to the United States.

Isadora separated from her husband on their return to Moscow in the summer of 1923, and a year later she left Russia. Although she did not know it at the time, she would never return there. The final years of her life repeated the familiar pattern. The harder she tried to pay her debts and raise money for a school, the farther back she seemed to slide. In 1927 she died in France as her children had—in a car accident.

One summer evening Isadora was invited to go riding in a sports car she had admired. She loved fancy cars and fast driving. "Good-bye, my friends. I'm going to glory," she cried in French, as she stepped into the car and wrapped her shawl around her shoulders. The car started and then stopped with a jerk. The shawl had caught in the spokes of the wire wheels, breaking Isadora's neck. The red shawl that she used in many of her performances had killed her.

Isadora was a pioneer, but not in the way she had intended. The Duncan school in Moscow finally became a school of acrobatics. Only a few dancers today perform in Isadora's style, and those who do imitate her dances rather than experiment with new forms.

Her theory of dance was to have its greatest effect on ballet, the very form against which Isadora had rebelled. She performed for some of the great ballet choreographers in Russia and Western Europe. She inspired them to combine her natural, graceful style with the formal movements and postures of ballet and to set dances to classical music. Hers was a dance that came from the human spirit and from great music. Like a prophet, Isadora Duncan brought new life to dance in Europe. Some who came after her in the United States would do the same for dance in their own country.

SPELLBINDER

MARTHA GRAHAM: She has shown us a new way of seeing ourselves in the beauty of her dance.

A bright spotlight picked out the single chair placed in front of the curtain. Swiftly, if a little stiffly, Martha Graham appeared and perched on the chair. The audience cheered. She had not said a word, and she was not expected to lift a foot to dance. But those in the audience knew what she had done, and they had come to pay tribute to her. It was 1976, and the program was a celebration of an event that had taken place fifty years earlier—Martha Graham's first modern dance recital.

When the theater became quiet at last, the tiny, dark-haired woman spoke softly into her throat microphone. The people leaned forward to hear her, just as she leaned forward in her chair. The house lights had not been dimmed, she told them, so that she could see their faces. She needed to feel that she was in touch with them. Her voice, surprisingly young for an eighty-one-year-old woman, reached each person with such warmth that everyone there felt that she spoke to him or her alone.

She talked about *Diversion of Angels,* one of the dances the company was to perform. "It's about love," she said. "All of my dances are about love, for that is all that matters." Then she introduced *Lamentation,* a dance that expresses grief. Love, grief—these themes touched everyone in the audience. They knew exactly what she meant, for they had known these feelings, just as we all do.

What makes Martha Graham a great artist is that she has put the feelings of all of us into a dance that is dramatic, powerful, and brand new. The story of her life is the story of modern dance.

Martha Graham did not begin to study dance until she was twenty-two years old. The oldest daughter of Dr. and Mrs. George Graham, she was born in Allegheny, Pennsylvania, in 1894. The people in Allegheny led lives that were as neat and orderly as the streets of their town.

Little in Martha's childhood hinted that one day she would become a dancer except for what she calls her first dancing lesson. To avoid a scolding for having done wrong, she had lied to her father.

"Martha, you are not telling the truth," Dr. Graham said.

She stared at him. There was no way that he could have known. "How did you know?" she whispered.

"There is always some movement that tells me you are deceiving me. Your back gets very straight. Maybe you shuffle your feet. Your eyelids drop. Movement does not lie."

The truth of her father's remark stayed with Martha, and years later, she based a theory of dance upon it.

In 1908 Dr. Graham moved his family to Santa Barbara in the hope that the warm, dry California sunshine would help little Mary's asthma. Today Martha says that the move west made possible her life in dance. In Santa Barbara there was space. Martha found space for the mind as well as the body in the land that swept from the mountains to the ocean. Gardens were lush with tropical plants, and the people, Chinese and Mexicans among them, had customs as colorful as the flowers. The soft lilt of Spanish hovered in the air, and on the Chinese New Year, a paper dragon twisted and turned through the streets.

When Martha first started going to Santa Barbara High School, she was shy with the other students and spent much of her time reading. But it did not take long for her to be caught up in school life. Soon she was dating boys and enjoying parties and dances. If there was anything unusual about this slight, large-eyed teenager, it was that she did everything she tried so well. Her strength and energy more than made up for her lack of size in sports. By the time she was a sophomore, she was captain of the girls' basketball team.

And then, one summer day, Martha's father gave her a bouquet of violets and took her to Los Angeles to see a dance recital by Ruth St. Denis. The dances swept from India to Egypt in bright flashes of silk and jewels with the tall, graceful figure of St. Denis moving at their center. Martha was enchanted and in a few short years she herself would become a part of the magic that was created for her that afternoon.

By the time Martha graduated from Cumnock Junior College in 1916, Ruth St. Denis and her husband,

Ted Shawn, had opened a new school in Los Angeles. The Denishawn School offered a program of "total dance." In addition to the basics of ballet, there were classes in oriental dance, Spanish dance, and any other kind of dance that happened to interest St. Denis and Shawn at the time. Martha leaped at the chance to study under St. Denis.

Her classes did not turn out the way she had expected. St. Denis saw the school mostly as a place to teach and work out new dances when she was not on tour. And she saw little promise in an awkward young woman named Martha Graham.

Ted Shawn saw something in her efforts, however, and Martha began her study of dance in earnest at the age of twenty-two. She was not only older than most of the other students, but she also had less training. Martha watched their graceful, fleet-footed movements closely so that she could learn from them. In his book about her life, *Frontiers of Dance,* Walter Terry tells us how her hard work paid off.

One day, while Martha was watching advanced students rehearse a Spanish dance for a performance, Ted Shawn glanced at her.

"It's too bad Martha doesn't know this dance," he remarked. "She would look just right in it."

Martha blurted out, "But I do know it."

"Impossible. You've only just seen it and never danced it."

Martha stepped onto the floor and danced. Shawn looked at her without speaking when she had finished.

"Was it that bad?"

"No, it was thoroughly professional in every way. You'll do it!"

From that time on, Martha was on the professional

Martha in an East Indian costume during her days as a Denishawn dancer.

side of the studio. She performed with the Denishawn Company and taught some classes herself.

She was only five feet two, and yet even then she could give the impression of great power on stage. Her slender body thrust and dove. Her big, dark eyes and high cheekbones suited her for proud, passionate, and even savage parts. By 1920 she had swept beyond other Denishawn dancers as a performer.

During 1922 and 1923 Martha toured widely with the Denishawn Company in both England and the United States. Then she was invited to star in the Greenwich Village Follies, a musical variety show that had one production after another on Broadway. The time had come for her to leave Denishawn. She was clashing with Ted Shawn regularly. He wanted things done his way, and Martha was hoping to find hers. She was also unhappily in love with Louis Horst, Denishawn's musical director. He was a married man, ten years older than she, who would later become her closest friend.

Martha danced in the Follies for two years before she found what seemed to be a way to try out her own ideas. The Eastman School of Music hired her to teach in its new department of dance. Soon she was teaching part-time at Eastman so that she could take a second teaching job at the Anderson-Milton School in New York City.

Teaching at Eastman was not what she had hoped for, since once again she was working with other people's ideas for the dance. She and her students were expected to do dances based on themes suggested by Eastman's director for schoolwide performance. But the spark that had first shown itself in her dancing for Denishawn drew people to her. Three young women who were students at Eastman wanted to join her in a dance company of her own. Louis Horst, who had left Denishawn to study musical composition in Europe, wanted to join her, too. He had discovered that composing music for itself was not for him. The idea of choosing, arranging, and writing music for dance, however, excited him. He had seen a different kind of dance in Germany that had hinted at what might be possible. And he believed in Martha Graham.

With Louis at the piano, Martha and her three young students gave her first dance recital on April 18, 1926, in New York City. She left the Eastman School in June and turned her back forever on performing other people's dances.

During the day, she taught dance at the Anderson-Milton School. Louis played for classes there and for musical shows and other dancers' recitals. Any money left over from basic living expenses went to pay for recitals. At night, Martha went to her studio to meet with her own dancers. The studio was home, too. She slept there on a narrow cot.

Her first three students were replaced with others who made their living during the day and practiced with her at night. They were paid only for dancing in the rare recitals—ten dollars a recital. They worked for Martha and the new form of dance that was slowly taking shape in her studio. "Martha was a witch," one of them has said, "and we were under her spell."

If Martha was a witch, Louis was a wall, and that is how he spoke of himself. There was no question of anything else but dance in Martha's life now, but Louis was there, and she leaned on him. He helped to pay her bills, kept her spirits up, and even scolded her when he thought she needed it. Most important, he let her know how he felt about her dance and how it was growing.

Course, *a dance first performed in 1935 by The Dance Group.*

By 1929 she had found her own way to speak through dance. *Heretic,* her first great dance, was performed in April, and nothing like it had been seen before.

Imagine a row of women, all dressed alike in dark, long, shapeless gowns, with great, black eyes staring blankly out of masklike faces. Their bare feet are pointed straight ahead, and they seem to be planted firmly in the earth. Three times a figure in a white gown tries to break through the wall, but each time the women regroup and drive her back. The third time, they turn away from the outsider with pounding heels, and she sinks to the floor, defeated.

Heretic was dance stripped to its barest. There were no sets, and the music was a simple folk tune played over and over. But its very plainness showed what being an outsider feels like.

In a book of drawings by one of her students, Martha refers to "the dancer's innerly felt world. This is not a world of ideas, but rather a world deeper. . . a world of precise awareness in terms of bone and nerve and sinew of the various acts which are emotions."

It was true that while the honesty of her dance put a small group of admiring New Yorkers in touch with their feelings, others thought it drab and dull. The great ballet master, Michel Fokine, told critic Walter Terry what he thought of it—"Ugly girl makes ugly movements on stage while ugly mother tells ugly brother to make ugly sounds on drum. That is Graham's modern dance." Fokine was no friend of Martha's however. She had enraged him during a press interview when, without knowing who he was, she told him to his face that he knew nothing of movement!

Martha suffered from criticism of her work, and at times she herself had doubts about its value. Was she saying what she meant to say in her dance? Would the audience understand? Sometimes she grew so weary and uncertain that she would lie on her cot and bury her head in her pillow.

At these times, Louis, who accompanied every practice session and class, was there to encourage her and to push her gently back to work. Martha had no private life to turn to for comfort. Dance was her life.

During the summer of 1930 they traveled to the West Coast. After performing in Seattle, they went to Santa Barbara, where Martha visited her mother, a pattern she tried to repeat each summer. On the way back to New York, they rested for a few days in Santa Fe, New Mexico. It was Martha's first visit there, and she was so inspired by the blending of Spanish and Indian culture that she made up two new dances based on it. The New York critics liked the southwestern dances, and they began to follow her work eagerly. What would she compose next? She was credited with creating, if not something beautiful, at least something that was interesting.

During the 1930s, people in the arts began to take notice of Martha Graham. She appeared as The Dancer in *Electra,* a Greek tragedy that looked forward to her own use of Greek myth in dance. She also did the stage movement for two plays produced by the noted actress, Katharine Cornell. She and her company, now known as The Dance Group, even appeared in the star-studded opening of Radio City Music Hall! And on February 26, 1937, at the invitation of Eleanor Roosevelt, she danced at the White House.

Summers she spent teaching at Bennington College, where Martha Hill, a former member of The Dance Group, had organized a dance festival. The Bennington

Festival became a summer home for modern dancers, and it helped train new people in modern dance methods. Most of the newcomers were physical education teachers from colleges and universities. In the fall they returned to their schools and included modern dance in their classes. In this way, many young women learned about modern dance in its early years, and Martha Graham's Dance Group was welcome on college campuses throughout the country.

One warm spring day in 1938 a young ballet dancer named Erick Hawkins came to Martha's studio. He asked if he could sit in on the rehearsal, and to everyone's surprise, Martha agreed. He was a new breed of dancer, one who was not so devoted to ballet that he would not study any other type of dance. He felt that Martha's technique might be helpful to him. Within a month he had been accepted into the Group, and the dance Martha was rehearsing, *American Document,* was redone so that Erick could be her partner.

Giving Hawkins a major role caused grumbling among the others. Martha had never allowed the dancers to bring their husbands to rehearsal, and now the first male dancer to join them had an important position. He even instructed the others while Martha worked on her solos. Dancers who had been with Martha for five or ten years did not like it, and four of them left her. It was the end of an era for The Dance Group, which became the Martha Graham Dance Company as more male dancers were added.

But it was a beginning, too. With *American Document,* Martha's dance took a new direction—one that required both men and women. She was creating what has been called a "dance theater." The dance had a plot and a script, which Martha wrote. Having reduced her dance to its barest meanings, now she was rebuilding it in her own way with the riches of the theater—sets, costumes, and the human voice.

In *Frontiers of Dance,* Walter Terry quotes Martha as saying, "I'm afraid I used to hit audiences over the head with a sledgehammer because I was so determined that they see and feel what I was trying to do. Now I know that you don't hit them as I first did or throw roses at them as some entertainers do, but that you must draw people to you, like a magnet."

American Document did draw people to it, and many were those who had little interest in pure dance. The performance in Carnegie Hall was sold out, and when the company went on tour, twenty-five hundred people came to see it in Chicago.

Audiences were more than ready for her next great dance, *Letter to the World,* presented in 1940. It was based on the life of Emily Dickinson, a major American poet. Like *American Document,* it had a script, in this case lines of Dickinson's poetry that Martha had chosen to express through dance. But once again, she tried something new that would appear in her later work. Dickinson had been a quiet, shy woman who for many years even refused to walk outside her home and garden. Her poetry, however, shows that she had a deep understanding of the human mind and its ties to the world. Martha used two people to show the poet's outer and inner lives. "She Who Speaks" was the prim New Englander Dickinson appeared to be. "She Who Dances" was the poet's passionate inner self. And with them swirled the memories, loves, and fears of the mind itself in dance.

Letter to the World drew more people to her dance, and newspaper reporters learned that Martha Graham was a charming woman. She cheerfully gave them her opinion on jitterbugging—"ugly beauty"—and fashion. Her love of beautiful clothes was a carryover from her dance, for which she designed and sewed many of the costumes. Agnes de Mille has called her "one of the great costume designers of our time."

In 1944 the last major dance in her American cycle burst upon the world. To this day *Appalachian Spring* is many people's favorite. Aaron Copland won a Pulitzer Prize for its beautiful music. Fittingly enough, the music was untitled for some time after it was written. Copland had scrawled over the cover, "Martha's music."

Appalachian Spring is Martha's dance at its most joyful. It is a celebration of the American frontier and of life itself. When it was first performed, Martha took the role of a young bride. At fifty, she ran on stage with all the beauty, happiness, and energy of a girl. She delighted in her new home, greeted her guests, listened to the preacher, and was swept up in the arms of her young, handsome husband, played by Erick Hawkins.

The love between men and women had been shown in Martha's dance for some time, and it had its place in her own life, perhaps because after those first hard years there was now a space for it. She shared her life with Erick Hawkins as openly as she did her dance. Shortly after they met, he had moved into her apartment, and their feelings for each other were tender and stormy by turns.

Two such strong-minded, talented people living and working together were bound to clash. Erick was fifteen years younger than Martha, and she was fast becoming a legend. He was eager to try out his own ideas and to help the company, but no one, not even her lover, could challenge Martha's control. After seven

Martha as a happy, hopeful young bride in Appalachian Spring.

years, Erick moved out of their apartment and stopped teaching classes at the studio.

Tensions were also building up between Martha and Louis Horst. During a difficult rehearsal in the 1948 summer workshop, he broke in several times to correct the student orchestra. His nerves were on edge, and he was irritable with his students. Finally, Martha told him, "Louis, this has got to stop."

Stunned, he looked up. She had criticized him in front of his music students. Without saying a word, he put down his baton and left the room. The same day he wrote a letter in which he resigned as music director. A working partnership of more than twenty years had come to an end.

After the workshop was over, Martha and Erick went off alone together to the Southwest. It was a place they both loved. Over the years, in fact, Martha had based some of her important dances on the moods of the countryside and the thoughts of the people there. It was a peaceful time for just the two of them, away from the pressures of the company. Without telling friends or family, they were married in Santa Fe on September 7, 1948.

In spite of its fame, the company was having financial problems. After they had been unable to afford a New York season for two years, Erick decided that something must be done. He was impatient with what he saw as Martha's lack of interest in business matters. Taking the last of their money to pay for his trip and without telling Martha where he was going, he left New York on a fund-raising mission. His efforts made the 1950 season possible, but Martha was so annoyed that she refused to give him billing outside the theater.

Although Erick deserved credit as her partner, he

ignored the gesture. He had bigger things in mind—a European tour sponsored by Bethsabee de Rothschild, a wealthy patron of modern dance. Martha was worried. She felt that Europeans, long used to ballet, might not like modern dance. She never had the chance to find out. She twisted her knee during the first performance in Paris so badly that the cartilage was torn. Since there was no one in the company to take her place, Erick quickly put together a program of dances that did not include parts for Martha.

The company went right to performance the next day and proved that Martha was right. Parisians had no use for modern dance, or at least, for the dance they saw. The concerts in Paris had to be cancelled.

When they went on to London, Martha pushed herself and rehearsed. Although she was in great pain, she was going to perform. Erick did not believe that she could do so and cancelled the tour. Martha was furious. After all, the tour had been his idea! They quarreled as they had never done before and hurt each other so deeply that their marriage was destroyed.

Without Martha to hold the company together, the dancers scattered and gradually worked their way back to the United States. Alone, Martha retreated to Santa Fe, where she had been married two years earlier. Without surgery it seemed that little could be done for her, but she refused to have an operation. She also refused to allow the injury to end her life in dance. One doctor described what was wrong in such a way that she could decide on her own treatment. She began lifting weights, and week after week passed as she exercised her weakened leg. Slowly she added more weight until her leg was strong enough to lift twenty-five pounds. Now she had to find out if she could dance again.

She danced for the first time the following spring, and within two years she had rebuilt her company into one of the best ever assembled. Her dancers understood her vocabulary of movement so well that often she had only to suggest an idea or a feeling for them to work out the movement. The 1953 spring season turned into one of her finest. Her knee was healed, and once again she commanded the stage.

During the 1950s the State Department chose the Martha Graham Dance Company to represent the American arts in other countries. Naturally, Martha was pleased, but she was worried, too. The 1950 tour was still a fresh memory. The company opened in London to halfhearted interest, but by the end of their time there, the British had warmed to modern dance. After stops in Holland, Belgium, Sweden, and Denmark, they went to Paris, where Martha had been injured four years earlier. The theater was filled with people eager to see her dance. The press was friendly, and Martha was hailed as a great artist when she received a diploma and medal from the city of Paris. At last, she had a following in Europe as well as in the United States. She returned to learn that the State Department had booked a tour to the Far East and Mid East on the basis of the warm response in Europe.

In late 1955, Martha, twenty-three dancers, and an orchestra took off for Japan with enough costumes, scenery, and technical equipment to fill two planes. Again Martha was worried. What would Asians, whose dance traditions were thousands of years in the making, think of modern dance? She should not have worried. By the end of the first week of performances in Tokyo, the audience nearly prevented the company from leaving the stage. On through the Philippines, Indonesia, India,

Martha in Clytemnestra, *a dance masterpiece in her Greek cycle.*

and Israel they danced. Some of the company began to suffer from exhaustion and illness, but not Martha. At sixty-one, she seemed to have her energy and well-being fueled by dancing for adoring audiences. Martha had circled the globe and left a trail of understanding for modern dance.

Not long after the State Department tour, she undertook her most ambitious dance, the opera-length *Clytemnestra*. Very few choreographers have ever dared to create a work so demanding.

It was the high point of a Greek dance cycle that Martha had perfected over the years. In these dances she dealt with ancient legends by exploring the thoughts and dreams of the central character. Now she took on the story of Clytemnestra, the tortured queen who killed her husband and was in turn killed by her son. The first part of *Clytemnestra* presented her as danced by Graham in Hades, the afterlife of the ancient Greeks. Then the dance looked back over Clytemnestra's life to probe the reasons for her troubled spirit. As soon as she remembered her past, another, younger dancer took over the role while Graham stayed on stage. It was done so skillfully that the audience was scarcely aware of it.

Martha was very much aware of it. Her body was growing older, and no longer could she force it into the spectacular movements with which she had founded modern dance. In the years to come, she would have to leave the dance as a performer. It would be a terrible parting.

"A dancer's instrument is his body bounded by birth and death," she had written years earlier. "When he perishes his art perishes also. . . . The world has only a legend about the individual, and the quality that has made him an artist."

Martha's choreography grew out of a dancer's experience with her own body in motion. No wonder she would not believe those who told her she was still a great choreographer. No wonder she would have nothing to do with her company's efforts to bring back her earlier dances. During a 1965 revival of *Primitive Mysteries,* one of her first great works, she sat alone and silent in her dressing room with one of her assistants, listening to the music and holding his hand. A year later, *Clytemnestra* was dropped from the repertory because she could no longer dance it.

The brilliance of her new dances dimmed as her strength failed, and by 1970, the Martha Graham Dance Company had a bitter choice to make. The Brooklyn Academy of Music offered to sponsor a series of concerts, but only if certain of her earlier dances were performed. They were dances that she could no longer perform and refused to bring back. By now the company was set up so that Martha's agreement was not necessary. A story in the *New York Times* predicted her retirement, and the company went on without her. On opening night she received the Handel Medallion, New York City's highest award in the arts. Her speech, in which she said she would retire in her own good time, moved the audience to laughter and tears.

The company needed her leadership, but Martha was unable to give it. Drinking was doing to her body what age did not, and her health was failing. During 1971 she was so ill that more than once her friends expected her to die. Her company tried to hold itself together by presenting studio performances. Under the guidance of older dancers who had learned the dances from Martha, they painstakingly brought her work back to life themselves.

And then, in 1973, Martha Graham returned to a new life in dance, one in which she would no longer perform. In March she called a press conference to announce that her company would have a two-week season on Broadway. Someone had once warned her, she told reporters, that she was not an immortal goddess. "That's difficult," she confessed, "when you see yourself as a goddess and behave like one. In the end I didn't want people to feel sorry for me. If I can't dance any more, then I don't want to."

Now Martha herself was going to make sure that her dances would be remembered. She revived *Clytemnestra* for the 1973 season and created two new dances for a season that promised, in the *New Yorker's* words, "a new dawn." And it was.

Since then, the genius of her dance has proved that it does not need her dancing to succeed. At eighty, she set out on another Far East tour sponsored by the State Department. Rudolf Nureyev, the famous ballet dancer, came to her studio to learn from her. She created a new dance, *Lucifer,* especially for him, and he brought to it a drama matched only by Martha Graham's own performances.

In 1976 Martha celebrated her fifty years in modern dance with gusto. She planned a new dance, she toured the country, and she received a steady stream of visitors at her studio. One of those who came to see her was Betty Ford, then First Lady and a former Graham student.

Now, perhaps more than ever, her power as a great creator of dance is felt by those who know her. In a recent interview in *Dance Magazine,* Tim Wengerd, a member of the company, talked about what it is like to work with Martha Graham. "Martha's vision is so strong

Martha on stage in 1976 with Betty Ford, who was then First Lady.

that it's a new world every time you go on stage. I have to dance one of her roles many times before I feel like I even have an inkling of what it really is about, what it really means, for each performance is a time of discovering something new, going deeper and deeper into the part. And that's the fact of Martha's dancing."

In her own words, "You have to gamble with your possibilities." Martha Graham has gambled all her possibilities on dance, and in doing so, has opened our eyes to a new way of seeing ourselves.

BALLET MEETS BROADWAY

AGNES DE MILLE: She so changed the role of dance in the theater that Broadway was never the same again.

When Agnes de Mille met with Richard Rodgers and Oscar Hammerstein II about a new Broadway musical, it was the most important job interview of her career. The year was 1943, Rodgers and Hammerstein were the most famous composing and writing team of the time, and the play was *Oklahoma!* Agnes wanted to be dance director, and she knew that the two men had doubts about her ability to handle the job. Even so, her voice was strong and firm when she told them that if she was going to compose the dances, the dancers in the chorus had to meet her standards. Too often in the past, she had been forced to work with poor dancers who were hired only because they were friends of the producer or director. Every one of these shows had ended in failure for Agnes.

She got the job and was given five weeks to create and rehearse the dances. In two weeks she had choreographed, or composed, forty minutes of dance. The routines seemed to spill out of her. Using two dancers as her assistants, she ran three rehearsals at once. And her work was just beginning.

Before a play opens on Broadway, it is tried out in other cities. If the people there don't like it, changes are made between performances. A play with serious problems may close before it even reaches Broadway.

In March the show opened in New Haven, Connecticut. In the audience were agents and drama critics who had come up from New York to review the new play. "Not very successful," the critics wrote.

The show moved on to Boston. Aboard the train Agnes met with the rest of the staff to redo the second act. She was asked to compose a new dance in one day, and somehow, she did it. The cast gave only a fair performance in Boston, and again, the critics were not impressed. But the audiences loved the show, and soon all performances were sold out. Maybe, just maybe, they had a hit.

After two more weeks of rewriting, they headed back to New York. At the Broadway opening, Agnes stood numb with terror behind the last row of seats. The curtain swept up on a woman churning butter while the baritone sang, "Oh, What a Beautiful Morning." After the last note, a sigh rippled over the audience. Agnes could feel them open their hearts, ready to enjoy whatever came next.

The ballet in the second act stopped the show while the audience roared with approval. Never before had they seen such a beautiful dance routine in a play.

It was a first for the musical stage and is Agnes

The 1943 production of Oklahoma! *that took Broadway by storm and brought fame to Agnes de Mille.*

Twelve-year-old Agnes in costume for one of her garage theatricals.

nothing until Margaret developed fallen arches. The doctor recommended ballet as treatment. To Agnes's delight, both sisters were sent for lessons to the Theodore Kosloff School of Imperial Russian Ballet.

Agnes was in her glory. Although at thirteen, she was rather old to be starting ballet, she didn't care. "I had found my life's work," she wrote later.

Agnes started every lesson the same way—heels together, feet turned out in the first position. Then, holding the barre, she did *pliés,* or knee bends, just as ballet students had started practice for three hundred years.

Agnes worked at class until sweat beaded her forehead and every muscle ached.

"May I sit down?" she asked.

"Never!" answered her teacher. "It ruins the thigh muscles."

At home Agnes doubled the number of pliés. She begged to have a daily practice session at the studio like the other girls in the class.

Her mother, however, thought one weekly private lesson and one class were quite enough. She did give in to Agnes's request to have a barre installed in the bathroom. Practicing alone, Agnes made and repeated mistakes, which became a real disadvantage to her.

Movements in ballet are not natural, and so they must be learned correctly. The dancer must exercise her legs to make them much stronger than normal. The rest of the body, too, must be trained to get the proper line, which is as important as the right movement.

For Agnes, whose body was long in proportion to her short arms and legs, getting the right line was very hard. Embarrassed in class because she had learned bad habits practicing alone, Agnes crept to the back row.

As a student, her best wasn't good enough for classic ballet.

She felt as if she was the clumsiest student in the class. She did have one talent, perhaps left over from her acting. She could pantomime. She was so good that Kosloff singled her out to demonstrate for the class. Pantomime remained one of her strengths. Since ballets often "tell" a story, it is an important gift for a dancer.

By the time Agnes graduated from high school, she was very discouraged with her lack of progress at the Kosloff School. She wanted to become a professional dancer, but she did not know where to turn. Her parents urged her to go to UCLA, the University of California at Los Angeles. She graduated from the university *cum laude* at the age of nineteen, an outstanding accomplishment. "And all I longed for was to dance the mazurka in *Sylphides* [a ballet with music by Chopin]," she remarks in her autobiography.

The day after Agnes graduated, her parents told her they were going to be divorced. It was a terrible blow. Agnes needed both of them at a time when she lacked direction and confidence in herself. "Stop dancing," her favorite college professor had told her. "You simply haven't a dancer's body." Agnes herself called the one production she had done for the Pasadena Playhouse "dreadful."

Anna de Mille and her daughters settled in New York where Agnes, overweight and out of practice, started daily exercises in a dance studio. The agents and producers for whom she auditioned were interested neither in the dances nor the dancer. There were two very important people, however, who came to believe in her ambitions. Her mother made the costumes for her New York debut in 1928, which Agnes had to finance herself. Her father sent her a telegram that read, "Welcome, my daughter, into the profession."

Two years later, William de Mille saw his daughter dance professionally for the first time. Agnes's mother had rented the Music Box Theatre in Hollywood for one performance. Agnes cared more about his reaction than the newspaper reviews and the rest of the audience combined. He arranged for another recital and invited all of his friends from the film industry. They complimented Agnes, patted her on the shoulder, and left. The doors of Hollywood were shut as tight as those of New York.

To keep up with new things going on in the field, Agnes went to private dance recitals. It was during this time that Martha Graham was trying to perfect a new form of dance. Agnes came to understand the importance of modern dance, and she and Graham became close friends.

"Martha, let me work with you," she asked Graham.

"Certainly, not," Graham replied. "Find your own way. I won't let you lean on me."

Agnes did find her own way. As she puts it in *Dance to the Piper,* "I turned my back on all I had done and faced the dark." She began working on dance composition rather than on the pantomime she did so easily. She wanted to hold the audience with steps, gesture, and movement rather than skillful acting. Ballet movement alone seemed tiresome. Agnes added elements of modern and folk dance to ballet, and this blending became a specialty of hers.

When word of a new musical, *Flying Colors,* hummed over the theater grapevine, Agnes decided to try for it. She and a partner, Leonard Warren, asked eight dancers to help, and Agnes choreographed a few routines. They won the audition, and she had her first job as a choreographer on Broadway.

Agnes went into *Flying Colors* with hopes flying. She soon found, however, that choreographing a Broadway show was far different from trying out her ideas with a few dancers in the privacy of a studio.

She has described choreography as being made up of two parts. First, one creates the patterns, steps, and gestures and then teaches the dancers to perform the dance. It is as if the choreographer is both composer and conductor, or dramatist and director, at the same time.

Agnes had worked only with small groups of dancers before. When she went into rehearsal for *Flying Colors,* she found it hard to plan dance patterns for the large chorus. Cast members and staff hovered about. They made her nervous, but she was too shy to ask them to leave. The stars changed a step here, a gesture there, and bit by bit took over entire numbers to show themselves off in the best light. Many of the dancers were hired for their beauty, not their dancing ability.

Just before the show opened, the set designer said that the chorus had to use a flashy, twelve-foot high platform for some of the numbers. It was dangerous, Agnes protested, and nearly impossible for the dancers to learn to use so quickly.

No one listened to her. When *Flying Colors* opened in September 1932, Agnes felt she had lost all control over the dances. The first performance flopped.

"Look," the producer said, "you've got to have five new dances in five days."

"I can't—I've lost my nerve," Agnes answered quietly. The producer knew she was right. He had already asked another choreographer to take her place. On the drive home Agnes watched the rain slide down the car windows and came to a new understanding of herself. Too many times in her life had she said yes to people when she really wanted to say no. The next time she would be firm about her rights.

Discouraged, disappointed, Agnes took a big chance. She left on a European dance tour paid for by her mother. It made no money, but as a result of it, she spent six years in London. She studied with Marie Rambert's group at the Ballet Club and performed with them at the Mercury Theatre. Working through misty, cold English winters and sweaty summers, she perfected her ballet techniques and became, at last, a truly accomplished dancer. "Thank you, America, for de Mille," wrote a London critic.

Midway through her stay in England, Agnes went home for a visit. Three years of study and successful performances had given her faith in herself. She would try to open those closed doors again. And try she did, in a big way. Her mother arranged for Agnes to perform at the Hollywood Bowl, one of the largest outdoor theaters in the United States.

Agnes got the Los Angeles Philharmonic Orchestra to play for the program and UCLA to furnish the costumes. Filling the huge stage, 104 feet across, proved to be a challenge. She choreographed dances ranging from jazz to opera and hired a cast of eighty. Late afternoon sun made the stage floor so hot that it blistered the dancers' feet during rehearsals. They cooled off in the grass and went on working.

The evening of dress rehearsal, everything seemed perfect. Orchestra, dancers, costumes, and lighting blended flawlessly. Agnes especially loved "Harvest Reel," based on American folk dances. She described dancing it at dress rehearsal—"I stretched out my arms in the moonlight and flew. I raced and raced in the cool night expanse on the largest stage in the world."

The actual performance promised to be just as perfect, but during the first number, the lighting engineer missed his cues. The stage was so dark that the audience could scarcely make out the movements. The engineer's booth was on a hill, too far away to be reached during the dance, and the number was totally spoiled. After the dim start, the audience of fifteen thousand grew restless. Even when the lights came up, the vast stage swallowed Agnes's choreography. The next morning one headline read, "De Mille Girl Fails." Agnes ached with embarrassment at failure in her home town.

Before she returned to England, she choreographed a musical, *Hooray for What*, whose title summed up her feelings about her career. It, too, flopped, but it taught Agnes the old lesson about the tough world of Broadway. She had to have control over the choice of dancers, and she had to be allowed to rehearse in privacy until the last step was planned.

Back in New York at the end of 1941, she looked long and hard at her career. It was hardly encouraging. She had a few dance students, but not enough to make a living wage. She had not made a reputation with the serious ballet companies. Broadway, she felt, was closed because of her earlier failures. Hollywood was no better. There was another choice. "I could quit," she decided.

Agnes made up her mind to apply for a job at Macy's department store. Yet from habit she continued to take classes at the Carnegie Hall ballet studios. Freed now of the need to excel, she could kick higher and jump like a child. A new excitement appeared in her dancing.

One day she heard along with other tidbits of ballet gossip that the Ballet Russe wanted an American work by an American composer. She went home and, fueled by many pots of hot tea, composed *Rodeo*, an

entire ballet based on some dances she had done in
London. She sent it off to the Ballet Russe and got the
job.

The Ballet Russe was filled with haughty Russians,
including Sergei Denham, the manager. They frightened Agnes, but she was no longer afraid of failure. She
had the courage even to leave the field of dance if she
had to.

She asked for Aaron Copland to compose the
music, because she thought he was the best.

She insisted on privacy for rehearsals until the
entire ballet was finished.

And she haggled with Denham over his right to
veto her work.

De Mille won.

Before Agnes started to work with the dancers, she
composed a general outline of movement. Listening to
the music, she "walked out" the entire ballet in her
studio. She needed to be on her feet to think in terms of
motion. When she started to work with the dancers, she
worked out the final steps and gestures, often inspired
by a movement of the dancers themselves. Agnes liked
to work with dancers who understood her "vocabulary
of movement." Just as language uses words, dance uses
a vocabulary of gestures, steps, and movements. Writers
develop a literary style, and choreographers develop a
style of movement.

Rodeo rehearsals took place during the summer of
1942 while the Ballet Russe toured the West Coast. Each
night the company performed, and in the afternoon they
rehearsed new works. It was sweaty and tiring, and
Agnes had to train the dancers to learn a whole new set
of movements. In *Rodeo* they had to bob and jerk as
though they were riding horses. Even walking had to be

Agnes and the noted American composer Aaron Copland take their bows after a recent performance of Rodeo.

relearned, and Agnes taught them the gait of a saddle sore cowboy. She herself kicked and jumped and bounced through the role of the lead cowgirl.

In September they returned to New York with only three weeks of rehearsal left. "In some ways this was the happiest period of my adult life," Agnes wrote in *Dance to the Piper*. "I was in love with the haunting legends of my land. I was also in love with a soldier."

The soldier was Walter Prude, a tall, slender young man from Texas whom Martha Graham had introduced to Agnes. To her, he seemed to be the best of Gary Cooper and the king of England, put together. Two weeks after they met, Walter had been drafted to serve in World War II. "Write me often," he told her. "Whether or not I answer, keep writing. This is important."

Agnes walked the streets of the city and thought about the upcoming performance. When she went back to her studio, she played the songs Copland had written for the ballet. The music recalled the land where Walter had grown up. As Agnes put it in *Dance to the Piper*, "I thought of the men leaving, leaving everywhere. . . . And what was left of any of them but a folk tune and a way of joining hands in a ring? And I searched my heart for the clues to remembering."

On opening night, October 16, 1942, the costumes arrived in a fleet of taxis only moments before they were to go on stage. Backstage, dancers warmed up with knee bends. The curtain swept up on the dark cavern of the Metropolitan Opera House. Agnes spit over her shoulder for luck and danced out. The music was too fast, so fast that she was breathless. Once she thought she would faint when her partner thrust her high into a lift and the blood rushed from her head. At the end she decided it had been awful. A good ballet but—she whispered to her partner—"a lousy performance." Then the applause began. Agnes was called back again and again for twenty-two curtain calls. It was her first real success.

Among those in the cheering audience were Richard Rodgers and Oscar Hammerstein II. "It turned out to be a rather spectacular way of getting an audition," she once told a reporter for the *New York Times*. Finally, those years of stubborn work paid off. She had a telegram from the Theatre Guild to come and see them the following week. This meeting began the talks that led to her becoming dance director for *Oklahoma!* and her brilliant career in the Broadway theater.

Nightly, Agnes reported on the ups and downs of *Rodeo* and *Oklahoma!* in her letters to Walter. Five days after *Oklahoma!* opened on Broadway, she took the train west to visit him. He had never seen her dance, and she went through every step in the show for him. When she left for New York, they were engaged, and in June 1943 they were married.

They spent their honeymoon in Hobbs, New Mexico, a hot, dusty air force base. While Walter went to the base each day, Agnes waited in a bare hotel room, going over the script of her next show, *One Touch of Venus*. In the evening she and Walter took long walks on the prairie that came up to the edge of town. She loved that— it was the same prairie of wide spaces that she had pictured for *Rodeo* and *Oklahoma!*

In the years that followed, Agnes choreographed a new musical nearly every year. In 1944 she had three hits running on Broadway at once: *Oklahoma!, One Touch of Venus,* and *Bloomer Girl. Carousel* followed in 1945. Starting with *Oklahoma!* a new breed of Broadway show appeared. Some critics considered it an entirely new theatrical art form. These large, spectacular musicals blended the best of a dramatic play with song and dance. They tended to be expensive, complicated productions. All of the staff—writers, composers, and choreographers—had to work closely together and blend their talents. Agnes was the foremost dance director in this new era of the theater. She also was the first female choreographer on Broadway and the first person to both choreograph and direct a musical. She directed the entire production of *Allegro* and shortly afterward choreographed and directed *Gentlemen Prefer Blondes*.

In late 1945 Walter came home from World War II and took a job as an assistant to Sol Hurok, a well-known music impresario who financed and booked concerts and shows. Agnes's and Walter's son, Jonathan, was born in 1946. Agnes wanted to continue her work, but Walter objected. In a recent *New York Times* interview, she said, "My career irritated my husband no end. I do care for him very intensely and give him as much time and attention as I can. But I could never sit home and play games. There's no game I've ever found. . . that is as interesting as my work." And elsewhere she has said, "I was greedy. I wanted wifehood and motherhood and work and I got them all."

Walter must have gone along, too, for they have had a long, lasting marriage. Thirty years after they were married, they were pictured dancing cheek to cheek in the *New York Times*.

Although she could earn large sums of money working on the Broadway stage, Agnes continued to compose ballets for serious dance companies, especially Ballet Theatre. One of her best-known ballets is based on the crime that inspired the jingle, "Lizzie Borden took an ax, gave her mother forty whacks. When she saw what she had done, gave her father forty-one."

Agnes was interested in why a young woman from a supposedly happy family would commit such brutal murders. She researched it as carefully as she rehearsed her dance steps. She went to Fall River, where the Borden family had lived, and interviewed people who knew Lizzie. She probed the mind and soul of Lizzie Borden in *Fall River Legend,* a tragic ballet that is far different from her Broadway shows. Lizzie Borden was never convicted in court for her parents' murders. She lived out her days in Fall River in disgrace. But Agnes judged her guilty and ended the ballet accordingly. Like *Rodeo, Fall River Legend* became part of the permanent repertoire of Ballet Theatre and has been performed many times over the years.

During the years that followed her Broadway hits, Agnes reaped the rewards of success. She was given the first look at scripts for musicals so that she could decide if she wanted to do them or not. She was asked to teach, lecture, and write about dance. Her energy seemed unlimited, and she did everything with the same quick intelligence and understanding that she brought to dance.

By this time Agnes had a style of choreography all her own. She repeated favorite movements and patterns in her dances. Except for circles, she never grouped dancers in geometric patterns. Often she had a dancer step on stage from one corner and then cross it diagonally. Thus a dancer entering at left front would exit at right rear. Many times one dancer would watch the others from one end of the stage. In rehearsal, she liked to keep all the dancers moving and on their feet. If one group rested while she worked with the others, time, attention, and money were lost. So while she was composing final steps and gestures on the spot, she had enough ideas prepared to keep everyone at work.

Working with some of the dance stars from her Broadway shows, Agnes formed the Agnes de Mille Dance Theater in 1953. Her dance company took to the road for twenty-six weeks, performing scenes and dances to classical music and folk melodies. They danced their way from the East Coast to California and back again.

When her work appeared on television, Agnes brought ballet to more people than would ever set foot in a theater or opera house to watch it. In 1956 she presented two programs, voted among the best on "Omnibus." The first program covered the history of ballet, and the second traced the history of dance from the earliest tribal rituals and religious dances to modern ballets. She has choreographed other original ballets and dances for television.

Agnes has always had an interest in financial support for the arts—especially the role the government might play. In 1965 President Johnson appointed her to the newly created Advisory Commission on the Arts. In 1970 she addressed Congress, pleading for continued support of the National Endowment for the Arts.

Skillful with words, she has written her autobiography and several books about dance. *Dance to the Piper,* the first volume of her autobiography, is translated into four languages and is the best-selling book ever written by a dancer. *And Promenade Home* and *Speak to Me, Dance with Me* are also autobiographical. *The Book of the Dance, To a Young Dancer,* and *Dance in America* are accounts of the history and technique of dance. They are a pleasure to read for their vivid, casual style.

When Agnes was in her sixties, a time when many people begin thinking about retirement, she began to plan a big, new project. She wanted to create a company that did nothing but American dances. And what better time would there be than the Bicentennial year?

She started in 1972, recruiting students from the North Carolina School of the Arts. She coached them in folk dances, particularly the kind found in Appalachia. She even taught them basic movements of workers, like the fancy footwork of a logger who tries to keep his balance on a log floating in water. Gradually, dances emerged from the movements, and they toured as the Heritage Dance Theatre in 1974.

By the spring of 1975 they were ready to present the program in New York. Agnes had arranged to give a lecture-demonstration with the performance. Standing backstage, giving last-minute instructions just before the performance, she suddenly lost feeling on her right side. She went limp and collapsed.

She had suffered a stroke—one that almost killed her. But even as she was being put to bed at the hospital, she said, "I'm going to be so bored."

She may have been bored, but being Agnes, she kept on trying. One year later she was up and about, needing a cane, but steadily improving. "I did worry that I might never have the use of my leg again," she told the *New York Times*. "But now I think I will, from the look of things."

On July 8, 1976, the American Ballet Theatre devoted an entire program to her dances—*Rodeo* and *Fall River Legend* among them. The mayor of New York gave her the Handel Medallion, the city's highest cultural award. Critic Clive Barnes commented in his review of the program that Agnes de Mille "has listened more than most—more than anyone—to the special sound of America dancing. She obviously feels America

The first performance of A Rose for Miss Emily, *which Agnes based on a short story by William Faulkner. Like* Fall River Legend *it deals with a murderer tormented by her guilt.*

in her feet, whereas most of us are lucky if we feel it in our heads." This, along with her skill as a choreographer and her genius in making dance a part of modern drama, is her gift to us. The gift would not have been possible were it not for her courage. In Barnes's words, "The woman has two qualities that very rarely come together. Guts and style. One without the other is easy. The two together is de Mille."

That she has both was shown once more in the spring of 1978 when she took up a dancer's most difficult challenge—a cross-country tour. She traveled with the Joffrey Ballet, presenting "Conversations about Dance."

During the evening-long performances, she remained onstage. In a style "as frisky as cats," to borrow one of her lines, she traced the history of all kinds of dance in America, while dancers from her own Heritage Dance Theater and the Joffrey Ballet demonstrated examples.

Because of her stroke, Agnes had no feeling in her right side and still needed to walk with a cane. But she was not paralyzed, and to prove it, she briskly raised her right arm high above her head during a press conference on the tour. "Months of therapy," she claimed. Not to mention guts and style.

Her latest book, *Where the Wings Grow,* was also published in 1978. It tells of Agnes's early summers spent at Merriewold, the de Mille country estate, before her family moved to Hollywood. It is a warm, witty, and deeply understanding remembrance of her childhood. In its last pages Agnes describes coming back to Merriewold with Walter. As she lay in bed listening to the well-loved nighttime sounds, it seemed that she was young once more. The book ends with her last thought before she fell asleep, "It was beginning."

PYMFFYPPM-
FYPNM YPF

TWYLA THARP: Her wit and daring speak to the young at heart.

Twyla Tharp stood at the sidelines of the rehearsal studio. Her right leg pumped to the music, dark eyes followed the action, hips rocked to the Beach Boys' beat. The choreographer was rehearsing her own dancers with members of the Joffrey Ballet for *Deuce Coupe*.

She stopped and barked out an order. "Look people, you're not articulating! Turn out! Use your feet all the way across." She jumped on a stool to get a better look.

The dancers started once more. This time a smile touched Twyla's little face. "That's right," she praised. "Good." Then, moments later she shouted, "You're still not slovenly enough!"

Slovenly? For a ballet? A ballet set to music by the Beach Boys? *Deuce Coupe* is not like any other ballet. It's about being a teenager, and it's one of Twyla's special blends of pop, modern dance, and ballet set to rock music. She shows things that teenagers like—boyfriends, girlfriends, surfing in the sun, and cars. And things they hate—pollution of the air and water.

It was 1973, and Twyla was rehearsing *Deuce Coupe,* her first major ballet. If she was nervous about its being accepted by an audience used to classic ballet, she didn't show it. What did make her nervous was not having enough time to rehearse.

Dancers with a large company, like the Joffrey Ballet, had to rehearse other dances and go to company classes, too. *Deuce Coupe* was only one of several ballets scheduled for the spring season. Twyla grew impatient when it was difficult to get all of the dancers together. One day she was able to rehearse from nine in the morning until nine at night. It made her happy as a clam.

On opening night, March 1, 1973, a crowd filled the New York City Center Theater to the last row. The curtain swept up on five dancers moving to the Beach Boys' California sound, born out of the slap of a wave on a surf board. It brought Dennis Wilson, the Beach Boys' drummer, to tears. "The greatest moment of my life," he says.

Off to the side, Erica Goodman, a dancer dressed in flowing white chiffon, was going through classic ballet steps with a set little smile on her face. She went through them in alphabetical order, as if she had learned them out of a ballet dictionary. It was Twyla's way of gently poking fun at ballet.

Would the smart, "uptown" audience be insulted? A jazzy trio took over, while Goodman went on with her alphabet. Dancers dashed into the wings. More ran onstage a second later. Warming up to the new idea, the audience whistled and cheered. They seemed to think it was fine to set a ballet to rock music.

Twyla joined the dancers during some of the nineteen sections. They bugalooed, frugged, and go-go danced.

During "Devoted to You," the second section, six graffiti artists—kids who normally spray-painted subway trains—moved to the back of the stage. There they sprayed sheets of white paper that slowly moved downward to pile up on the stage. It was instant scenery. But the audience had to keep an eye on it or they would miss the drawings since paper and paint kept moving. Like Twyla's ballet, the action was fast.

When the last note died on "Cuddle Up," the final section, those in the audience rose to their feet. They clapped, yelled, and shrieked. "Delirious" wrote the *New York Times*. Twyla's ballet was the hit of the season.

Deuce Coupe focused attention on Twyla. People who had never gone to the ballet before, liked hers because of its music. Joffrey audiences liked the fresh approach to dance. Before *Deuce Coupe*, Twyla's name was known to a fairly small group of people interested in new, off-beat ideas in dance. Now her audience was much larger, and it would continue to grow. This was just the beginning.

Today she is in her mid-thirties, but her pointed, pixie face, topped with thick brown hair that stops just short of her eyelashes, makes her seem much younger. So do her loose, easy movements that can abruptly turn into dazzling turns and slides. Each dance is bold, unexpected, and like no other.

If Twyla's dances are unusual, so are other things about her, including her name. Just before she was born, on July 1, 1941, in Portland, Indiana, her mother read the name "Twila" in a newspaper. It belonged to the princess in a pig-calling contest at the state fair. Lecile Confer Tharp changed the spelling to "Twyla" for her daughter. She thought it would look better on a theater marquee.

Mrs. Tharp was a pianist who had studied to become a concert artist, and she had ambitious plans for Twyla. Ear training in music came first—when Twyla was just one year old. At two, her mother started piano lessons for her, outside of the home so she would take music more seriously. By the time Twyla was four, she was practicing two hours a day.

Violin lessons followed, and then she started dancing lessons—tap, acrobatics, and ballet. Twyla calls all the lessons her mother's "buckshot notion of education." Practice in dance was timed to the minute: ten minutes for ballet, fifteen minutes for tambourine dancing, twelve minutes for tap, and eleven minutes for handstands.

In the late 1940s the Tharp family, which included twin boys and a younger sister, moved to San Bernadino, California. Twyla's lessons continued. She moved on to viola and became very good at baton twirling.

From the time she was eight years old, Twyla also helped in the family business. Her father, William, ran a chain of drive-in movies. Twyla car-hopped and sold popcorn at the snack counter year-round until she was eighteen.

"For ten years, I saw four features and ten cartoons, every single week. Every single movie that Hollywood made in the 1950s," she remembers. "That was my only contact with the outside world."

Obviously, the pizzazz and slickness of show business, Hollywood-style, impressed her and appeared years later in her dances.

Twyla was as bright a student as she was talented at acrobatics and dancing. By the time she was in high school, she was being tutored in foreign languages not offered in her regular classes. During her sophomore year she went to junior college to take trigonometry, and she learned typing, shorthand and dictation as well.

In spite of all her activities, Twyla graduated first in her class and went on to college as a pre-med major. That may seem a surprising choice for someone who had years of dance and music lessons, but Twyla is full of surprises. After three semesters at Pomona College in California, she switched to Barnard College in New York City. She wanted to study dance in New York, although she did not think about dance as a career choice. At Barnard she majored in art history—she had had her fill of math after trigonometry, and she needed more math for pre-med.

Twyla must have believed her mother's buckshot theory of learning. She studied ballet with Igor Schwetzoff, and she went to Martha Graham's studio for modern dance. She studied with Erick Hawkins, Alwin Nikolais, and Merce Cunningham—a master teacher, she claims. Her well of energy seemed bottomless. She took five dance classes a day and finished her art history major at Barnard, graduating in 1963.

Although she still had almost no social life, she had met and fallen in love with another student. They married while she was still at Barnard. But the romance was short lived. She and her husband divorced soon after her graduation. It was then that she realized what she had missed by not knowing other teenagers while she was growing up. "I didn't know how to talk to anybody. I didn't know that other people had problems," she told an interviewer for *Rolling Stone*.

By this time she had made an important decision—
she was going to become a professional dancer. The
Paul Taylor Dance Company was her choice since Taylor, a modern dancer, had a style of moving that was to
her liking. Before long, the bright, lively young dancer
was singled out as an outstanding member of the company. During a European tour in the summer of 1964,
her picture appeared in a London newspaper, and in the
article that went with it, a critic chose her as his favorite.

Performing other people's dances did not hold interest for independent-minded Twyla very long. A year
later, she left the Taylor Company and went to work
selling perfume at Macy's department store. At night
she hunted for a dance studio.

Although Twyla claims she knew nothing about
choreography, she had her own ideas about movement
and about the kind of music she might use. Her first
dance was called *Tank Dive* and was done to "Downtown," a popular song of the mid-1960s, sung by Petula
Clark. *Tank Dive* had its first performance at Hunter
College in New York City in April 1965.

Clive Barnes, the *New York Times* critic, was not
as pleased as her small audience when he saw *Tank Dive*
that year. "She moves beautifully," he wrote, "but her
personal direction was too bland." It would take time
and many more dances to change his mind.

Twyla's direction is, in fact, firm, although she
urges her dancers to help in planning a dance. She shows
them a phrase—a short series of movements—and has
someone copy it. First it is imitated, and then it is tried
backwards, turned upside down, and done to double time
or half time. By the time a work is complete, it is perfect
in Twyla's eyes, and each dancer in the company has
helped to make it so. While her dances often look as if

Directing a rehearsal, Twyla looks completely absorbed and ready to spring into the dance.

they are made up on the spot, they are planned to the last knee bend and finger twitch.

One clue to her unusual style is to read her notes on the first few dances: "fouette, wiggle, wiggle;" "windmill arm jump;" "cross-across scootch." Twyla's movements are so original that she has to make up words to describe them.

By the late 1960s, two other dancers, Sara Rudner and Margaret Jenkens, had joined Twyla. The company of three did not limit themselves to doing dances for the stage. In fact, they usually performed in churches, college gymnasiums, and museums. In *Re-Moves,* which premiered at Judson Church in New York City, Twyla and her two dancers arranged themselves around a huge wooden cube. Sitting around three sides of the cube, the audience could see only the action in front of them. The dancers' entrances were bound to cause comment. Sara rolled in clutching the inside edges of an enormous hoop while another dancer climbed down on a rope ladder. All three held their faces as stiff as a mask during the entire dance, which wasn't really a dance, but just pure movement. The audience, who liked new, untried ideas, adored it. Clive Barnes didn't. "Miss Tharp . . . is so cool that she could use a refrigerator for central heating," he said.

In spite of his opinion, Twyla moved on to other shores and widened her circle of admirers. During early 1967 she, Sara, and Margaret went to Europe. "Just we three. No manager. No tech people. No nothing," is the way Twyla describes the tour. "We carried all the props ourselves, all the costumes, everything—from museum to museum."

In *Jam,* premiered in Amsterdam, the only lighting came from lamps that the dancers held themselves.

Twyla had stopped using music, so the audience heard only their breathing and their feet hitting the floor. The first audience to see another new dance, *One Two Three,* gathered in a museum in Stuttgart. In Paris, Twyla looked at the auditorium of the American Center and shook her head. The space would never do. "She put the chairs on the stage and we danced where the audience usually sat," Margaret remembers. "Twyla does not just accept what is there. She molds it to make it better for dance."

The three young women danced on to London before coming home. Home for Twyla often was her dance studio in downtown Manhattan. Although she also had an apartment near Columbia University, she often sublet it for extra money. "You can't eat the limelight," she says.

Money is always a problem for new dance groups, especially a daring one like Twyla's. Rose Marie Wright, who joined Twyla in 1968, earned money on the side by babysitting. She not only got paid, she also got a meal on the job. Often Twyla and her dancers earned as little as twenty dollars a week from their dance. One way that Twyla kept the company working was to take short dance residencies on college campuses. During these times she could compose her own dances while working with the students.

Twyla used almost anything for inspiration. When the *New York Times* printed an error with the unpronounceable spelling "Pymffyppmfypnm Ypf," Twyla used it for the title of a dance performed at Sullins College. She rolls the title off her tongue as though it's the easiest thing in the world to say.

Even though she had stripped her dances to bare bones—no props, music, or other effects, she did use lovely costumes. New ones were designed for each dance by Robert Huot, a painter and teacher of art at Hunter College in New York. Twyla's interest in Robert grew beyond the professional tie. They were married at the end of the 1960s. She is, however, silent about her personal life. "It's private," is her answer to curious questions. She wants the public to know her by her work. Period. In truth, her work, filling most of the hours of the day and night, is her life.

In five years of choreographing, Twyla had composed twenty-three major dances, an impressive output. She preferred creating new dances to performing her old ones. "You can keep on chewing gum for ten hours," she told an interviewer from *Ballet Review,* "but after about a minute and a half you've got all the good out of it."

During 1970 her husband was eager to get away from the New York art scene, and so he and Twyla moved to a farm in upstate New York. It was 250 miles from the city. Dancers kept drifting up to work, especially Rose Marie Wright, the six-foot dancer who is a mainstay of the company to this day. "I kind of grew up dancing with Rose," Twyla has said, "and Rose grew up dancing with me and that's something special."

Life on the farm was as fruitful as an apple orchard in August. Four dances came out of the summer of 1970. And Twyla became pregnant. Instead of letting that stop her, she danced to a Willie Smith record each day. She videotaped the dance to show the changes caused by her pregnancy. Parts of these tapes were later shown on the "Today" television show.

New ideas began to pop up. Twyla's interest in jazz and popular music dates from that summer on the farm, when she began to listen to records and read the

Trained in ballet and modern dance, Twyla's superb movements are all her own.

album covers. She started to use music for all of her dances at a time when it was stylish for new experimenters in dance to perform in silence.

The decision to use music was important, mostly because of the kind of music Twyla chose. She turned to jazz, and its rhythms changed the dances. They became more swinging, more slick, and had a show business look. The music made changes in the audience, too. People who had no interest in experimental dance liked the jazz pieces. Soon the small company began to perform more often—on a stage in a theater. During the early 1970s they repeated the jazz pieces, and each time the audience thought they were as fresh as a new stick of gum.

The year 1971 was an important one for Twyla. In the spring her son Jesse was born. "He's terrific, terrific," she claims happily.

This was also the year that she composed one of her most popular jazz numbers, *The Bix Pieces*. It was written to Bix Beiderbecke's music and had several parts, including a baton twirling act by Twyla. The dance was planned for premiere at the Paris Festival in the fall.

Before she left for Europe, Twyla showed the dance to some of her friends and dance critics. Afterwards, hot and sweating, she answered questions while she changed Jesse's diaper. Sara Rudner and Rose Marie Wright slipped in and out, bringing damp cloths and a warm bottle. Twyla juggled being a mother and dancer just as skillfully as she had managed art history and dance classes during her college days.

French reviews of *The Bix Pieces* were mixed. One newspaper called it "grotesque." Another gushed, "dazzling with verve and panache." American audiences and critics loved it. When Twyla and the dancers did *The*

Bix Pieces in New York the following summer, even Clive Barnes found it "thoroughly delightful." He wrote, "You can see her past, her tap dancing, her youth, her career, her baton twirling, probably even her mother. . . . Miss Tharp is a dancer-choreographer to be reckoned with." From this time on, Barnes was a fan of Twyla's.

Even more important than his opinion was the reaction of someone else in the audience. It was Robert Joffrey, director of the Joffrey Ballet. He was so impressed with the dance that he invited Twyla to choreograph a ballet. That turned out to be *Deuce Coupe,* Twyla's first big splash in the world of dance. The ballet became such a crowd pleaser that Twyla redid it to be performed by Joffrey dancers only. The new version is called *Deuce Coupe II* and is one of the most popular numbers in the permanent Joffrey repertory.

Although Twyla and her dancers performed more than ever in the early 1970s, earning a living from dance was still not easy. In addition to working for brief periods on college campuses, Twyla also applied for grants from the New York State Arts Council, the National Endowment of the Arts, and various private foundations. She grew impatient with the long, often detailed questions on grant proposals and often returned the forms blank with a note: "I'm sorry. I write dances, not application forms. Send me the money. Love, Twyla."

It must have worked, because she claims with pride that she and her dancers have never been in debt. In the spring of 1972 she received the Brandeis University Creative Arts Award, a financial boost and an honor. Twyla accepted the award that praised her and then responded in deadpan style, "I'm just too young to be receiving awards." She called for the two dancers who had been with her longest, Sara Rudner and Rose Marie

Wright. They bounded to the platform and Twyla immediately handed the money to them.

That year Twyla added the first male dancer, Kenneth Winkler, to her company. She did not use him as a "man" dancing with "women," but simply as another dancer. About this time she stopped going to the farm. It simply was becoming too difficult to work with people who lived 250 miles away in New York City. She must have had reasons of her own, too, for her marriage also came to an end. After seven years she and Robert Huot were divorced. Jesse continues to live with Twyla and spends summers with his father. Twyla has a friendly relationship with her ex-husband, who still designs costumes for her dances.

The success of *Deuce Coupe* led to another invitation for Twyla to do a major ballet for Robert Joffrey. Again she found rehearsal time with a big company hard to come by. In the fall of 1973, when she was able to work with the company, she concentrated on rehearsing the dances and still hadn't picked a title. Finally, someone from the publicity department told her, "Twyla, time is going by. The papers are screaming. We've got to have a title for your ballet."

Without taking her eyes off the rehearsal, she muttered, "Okay, call it 'As Time Goes By.' Now don't bother me."

"As Time Goes By" is the song that Hoagy Carmichael sang in the movie *Casablanca*. The song is not, however, part of the ballet. Instead Twyla chose classical music—the last two movements of Haydn's Farewell Symphony.

A story about the symphony provided the idea for the dance. At the time that Haydn wrote the symphony, he was working at the country home of the emperor of

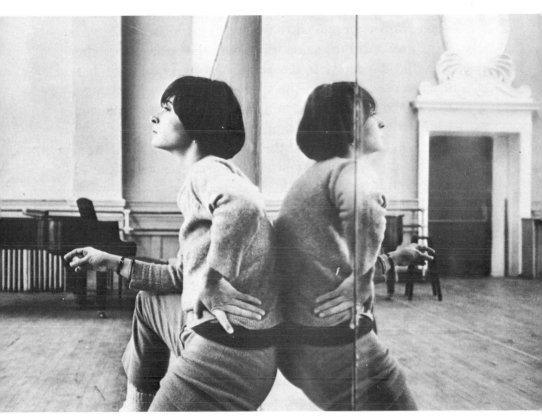

Twyla in her studio, where she spends her long working days.

Austria. The musicians of the royal court wanted to get back to their families in Vienna, so Haydn wrote the symphony as a hint to the emperor. During the last movement, the musicians blew out the candles on their music stands and walked away, one by one, until a single musician played to a dangling finish.

Twyla did the same thing with the ballet. Near the end, the dancers left the stage one by one. With her usual sense of humor, she sped up the farewell gestures in a dance joke. The curtain dropped on a single dancer while he was still in motion.

On opening night the audience went wild, and someone tossed a bouquet. Twyla grabbed it quick as a wink and tossed it back. The audience roared with laughter.

Following *As Time Goes By,* Twyla returned to jazz and pop music. She chose Fats Waller's lazy jazz for *Sue's Leg.* The duet for two couples was composed when her company was in residence at the Walker Art Center in Minneapolis in February 1975. The dance is named for Suzanne Weil, performing arts program director of the center. Later that year Twyla choreographed *Ocean's Motion* to Chuck Berry's beat.

Then she found a way to combine both classical music and pop in a single ballet. The work was choreographed for another company at their invitation. The company was the American Ballet Theater. Twyla had moved "uptown" about as far as you can go in the ballet world.

Everyone must have wondered what she would do for a company that specialized in *Giselle, Sleeping Beauty,* and *Swan Lake,* classic ballets all. Would she have them jerk, wiggle, or even blow big pink bubbles as Rose Marie Wright had done in *Ocean's Motion?*

Would they stamp on the floor and splat eggs as in some of the early dances of the 1960s?

Her first choice, to blend classic and pop music, was a stroke of genius for a company used to the classics and a choreographer used to working with pop music and dance forms.

Her second choice, to use Mikhail Baryshnikov, the darling of the company, in a leading role was just as inspired. Baryshnikov, who could move with rubber limbs and triple joints, was perfect for her fast-paced, quirky style. And his carefree sense of humor matched hers.

At the beginning of the ballet, called *Push Comes to Shove,* he swaggered out to the rinky-tink ragtime music of Joseph Lamb's "Bohemia Rag." Two ballerinas, who would usually have made their entrance wearing white tutus and posing in graceful arabesques, hammed it up in slinky dresses and joined him in a vaudeville dance routine.

The music switched to Haydn's 82nd Symphony. Baryshinikov plunged into a "serious" solo, then stopped in mid-turn and raked his fingers through his hair. The audience giggled. The rest of the dancers came on stage. They stumbled, reeled, and danced in triple time. The ballet seemed to be on the edge of becoming a complete mess, but it never did. Because Twyla understood the structure of dance so well, it had a strong skeleton of time, space, and motion.

"A hit," wrote Clive Barnes after its premiere on January 9, 1976. He called Twyla "a genius" and a "master chef." "You could only love it or hate it. I love it."

Not all critics did. Hubert Saal of *Newsweek,* not one to admire Twyla, commented icily, "It's modern, it's trendy, it's now, but it's not—like art—forever."

Never mind his opinion. *Push Comes to Shove* shoved Twyla to stardom in the world of ballet. Three years after its premiere, it is among the most popular dances in the American Ballet Theater repertory. It has been shown on television, amusing more people than ever.

While Twyla was having hard, five-hour rehearsals for *Push Comes to Shove,* she was also getting her own company ready for a ten-day season at the Brooklyn Academy of Music. "This is too much," she squealed, talking as fast as she dances. The tiny dancer ran from one rehearsal to the other, not even bothering to put jeans on over her patched practice clothes. She layered tights, leotards, and sweaters.

The Brooklyn appearance was the first real New York season that she had with her own dance company. When she had the program printed, she did not use the name, "Twyla Tharp Dance Company." She listed each of the dancers in the order that they had joined the company. After her own name came Rose Marie Wright, Kenneth Rinkler, Tom Rawe, Jennifer Way, Shelley Washington, Sharon Kinney, and Kristin Draudt. She dedicated the program to Rose Marie Wright. When she walked out on stage for curtain calls, her tiny form was hidden behind a great mound of six dozen roses that she gave to Rose Marie. It was her way of paying respect.

Twyla's new star status brought invitations from everywhere during the summer of 1976. She danced a duet with Baryshnikov in the American Ballet Theater gala and took her own company to Berlin and Edinburgh for summer festivals. Back in New York in the fall, her company joined the Joffrey for another ballet.

As usual her audience was in for a surprise. Twyla chose country music for *Happily Ever After*. She brought Sniffy Jenkins and Pappy Sherril and the Hired Hands, a blue grass group, from South Carolina and set them onstage behind a black sheer curtain. The country rhythms gave the dance a bigger, bolder, more sweeping look.

In the spring of 1977 a new Brooklyn Academy season summed up Twyla's career. It included dances with mathematical formulas and repeated phrases, pieces set in silence and to classical music, ballet jokes, and dances featuring country music and pop. Twyla danced a solo to *Fifty Ways to Leave Your Lover,* while songwriter Paul Simon himself played the guitar.

People everywhere were eager to see Twyla and her company. During 1978 they toured the country, an unusual event since they do not consider themselves a touring group. A year later, choreographing the film version of the musical *Hair* was another first for Twyla. Her casual patterns were new and exciting on the screen. *Time* compared *Hair* with the best movie musicals of the last twenty years.

Stardom seems to have made few changes in her personal life. More money has allowed her to move to a new apartment on Central Park West in New York City, but mornings still find her beating the rush hour as she takes an early subway to her studio. She stops only long enough to put away a breakfast fit for a line backer, let alone a woman who weighs barely a hundred pounds. Her work day begins in a loft four floors up in New York's garment district. She and her dancers work all day until everyone is hot, dripping, and thoroughly tired out. Then, it's time to go home to Jesse and a few special hours.

Twyla performing in Country Dances, *a recent country and western delight.*

Twyla's main social life centers on Jesse, as it has for the past several years. She gives him a big birthday party each year, complete with cake, friends, and lots of presents. For entertainment, Twyla enjoys a huge record collection.

She avoids celebrity hang-outs in New York, where she certainly would be welcomed as a superstar of the dance world. She is too busy for that kind of thing, and she prefers the company of people she knows best—usually those who work with her.

"The nicest time with Twyla doesn't happen when you meet her, but when you first see her respond to you as a person," explains Roddy O'Conner, her company manager and good friend. "She's very organized and disciplined, and at first you think you know her and that's all there is. Then comes a day when she lets something else out of the bag. Something vulnerable—and a really warm sense of humor."

The humor, of course, is right on the surface of her work, along with her understanding of all kinds of music and dance movement. Put together in her own way, it comes out as art, Tharpian art.

NEW STAR
RISING

GELSEY KIRKLAND: She first claimed fame at seventeen and is the ballet star of today and tomorrow.

Gelsey Kirkland stood at the barre, going through a set of exercises to warm up for rehearsal for her leading role in *Midsummer Night's Dream*. Concentrating hard as usual, she was interrupted. There was a telephone call for her. Little did she realize that it would change her career. And her life.

The call was long distance, from Toronto, Canada. There, just a few days earlier, on June 29, 1974, Mikhail Baryshnikov, the boy wonder of Russian ballet, had left his company while it was on tour. After a performance, he had walked to a bus that was to take the dancers back to their hotel. Suddenly, he bolted and headed straight for a waiting car. Soviet police traveling with the company chased the slight blond dancer. But Canadian police blocked their path and let him escape.

Now, because he could not speak English, he called Gelsey through a friend. "Would you be interested in dancing with Mikhail?" the Russian's spokesman asked.

"What do you mean, would I dance with him?" Gelsey screamed at the top of her voice. "Of course I will."

One of the most exciting dancers in the ballet world had invited her to dance with him at the American Ballet Theatre. It was exactly what Gelsey wanted to do. She was flattered that he had picked her above all other American dancers.

But it was frightening, too. Was she up to dancing with her famous partner? Was she good enough to share the spotlight as an equal? "I was very, very scared," she told John Rockwell in a *New York Times* interview. "But something overcame that fear—the sense that it was the right thing to do."

And so she set about leaving her own company, the New York City Ballet, and transferring to the American Ballet Theatre. Then, excited and nervous, she went to Canada to rehearse for her first performance with Baryshnikov. It would be the *pas de deux,* or dance for two persons, in *Don Quixote,* and it would be a good introduction to the type of ballet she would dance with him. They were story ballets that required her to act as well as dance. In spite of Gelsey's fears, the pas de deux went well.

Next came a much bigger challenge. They would dance *Coppélia,* a full-length ballet, for their American debut at the Kennedy Center in Washington, D.C.

She worked harder than ever until every step, every gesture was just right. Then she concentrated on putting them together. The eyes of the entire ballet world would be turned on the two of them.

Opening night was November 2, 1974. The audience, on pins and needles, filled every seat of the jewel-box opera house at Kennedy Center. Gelsey and Mikhail danced out as Swanilda and Franz, the village lovers of *Coppélia*. She had hardly done a *fouetté* or he a *jeté* before the audience saw that they were perfectly matched. Not only did they dance to perfection, they also appeared to be having fun as the two playful lovers.

Before the final note had sounded, the audience cried "Bravo!" and jumped to their feet. Gelsey and Mikhail bowed and bowed again. Someone gave Gelsey an armful of red carnations. In the traditional gesture she pulled one out and started to hand it to Mikhail. But then, she thrust the entire bouquet into his arms.

Mikhail looked astonished, the audience was delighted, and critic Clive Barnes wrote, "She could have melted like Jello in June. Instead . . . she matched him. She even challenged him. What was important was that they were dancing together as if they had grown up together. Perhaps they had."

At the time, Gelsey was twenty-one years old. She had already earned the name "child star" because of her fame at an early age and doll-like appearance. She had been a star with the New York City Ballet since she was seventeen. Working harder than most dancers, and with more will than most, she was a principal dancer at nineteen. She knew every ballet in the entire repertory of the New York City Ballet. Now she had the repertory of classic, fairy-tale ballets of the American Ballet Theatre to learn. And she would have to measure up each time she danced with the famous Russian dancer. Those were the kind of challenges that Gelsey liked, even though she sometimes nearly failed when she reached for things that were at the limit of her ability.

Gelsey at the carefree time in her life before she learned to dance.

Gelsey has always been serious about anything she tries. Her mother claims that she was born marching. The date was December 29, 1952, in Bethlehem, Pennsylvania.

She spent her early childhood in a rambling country house in nearby Bucks County. Her parents were associated with the New York theater. Jack Kirkland was a playwright and loved to entertain carloads of his theater friends in the big house. Gelsey's mother, Nancy Hoadley, was an actress and talented pianist. She was Jack Kirkland's fifth wife and much younger than her husband.

Besides Gelsey's older sister Johnna and her brother Marshall, several children from her father's other marriages lived with them, as well as some grandchildren. Gelsey did not quite fit in with the carefree ways of the big family. "Her seriousness was always a source

Gelsey's parents, Jack and Nancy Kirkland.

of kidding," says her brother-in-law, Don Bevan. "But she would never encourage it. She would never give the adults satisfaction."

When Gelsey was three years old, the family moved to New York City, their home before her birth. Although he had loved the country, Jack Kirkland thought it was time for his daughters, especially Johnna, to start preparing for careers in the theater. They settled into a roomy apartment on the west side of New York City, and the girls started taking different kinds of lessons. Gelsey became interested in ice skating and worked hard at doing it better than anyone. Her mother remembers her whirling around the Wollman rink in Central Park with her tummy sticking out and a frown on her face.

When Johnna was eight, she started to take lessons three times a week at the School of American Ballet. Gelsey often went to class to watch. "I guess my sister Johnna got me started," she later said when asked how she had started dancing.

After Gelsey's eighth birthday, she, too, auditioned for the ballet school. In those days she had a large stomach, small legs, and a big head. Standing nervously in a leotard, tights, and saddle shoes, she hung onto the barre as hard as she could. An instructor came up and lifted her leg to see how limber she was. Gelsey was so tense that she was brittle as a newly formed icicle. The other leg slipped out, and she plopped on the floor. It was an awful beginning, but she got into the school.

And what a school it was! Most of the ballet teachers had been dancers at the New York City Ballet. Many of them had come from Russia, like the head of the school, George Balanchine, or "Mr. B," as everyone called him.

Balanchine had started the School of American Ballet so that he could train dancers to do the kind of dance he likes—neoclassical ballets. Such ballets do not tell a story. They are simply made up of traditional ballet steps and movements set to music. This is Balanchine's "pure dance" style of ballet, done with quick, sharp movements. He learned the traditional steps when he was a student at the Imperial Ballet School in Russia. Now Gelsey was learning them in class.

She started each lesson in the same way—with knee bends, or *pliés,* at the barre. The teacher called out a set of barre exercises. Sometimes the order changed, but the exercises were the same, and they did all of them during every class.

Then Gelsey took her place at the center of the floor, where the class stood in exact rows. The teacher watched with a sharp eye and spotted even the tiniest mistakes. Only after Gelsey had gone through a whole set of floor exercises, did she move about the studio in something that looked like dancing.

She had to remember more than just the right exercises and movements. Her seat and stomach had to be tucked in, her chest held high, and her feet and legs turned out. Turnout was hard for Gelsey. It was the thing she had to keep in mind the most.

She learned that extension is important for a dancer. Her feet and ankles had to be stretched out in straight, sharp angles from her body. She and a friend, Meg Gordon, put on heavy rubber sweat pants to keep their legs warm. Then they took turns stretching each other's legs to improve their extension.

Gelsey's muscles were often tense. Sometimes as Meg pulled further and further, until Gelsey's knee touched her forehead, her legs hurt so much that she cried. But she was set on improving, on being the best in the class.

The fact that people compared the Kirkland girls made Gelsey uncomfortable. She was more shy than outgoing, bubbling Johnna. And she was more than two years younger, so comparisons made her worry. Could she ever catch up to Johnna? Would she ever be as good?

As she grew older, she fretted about her appearance. She thought her nose was too small and her eyes too large. Then she decided that she had a poor complexion. Photos, however, have always shown her to be pretty with long silky hair, large eyes, and perfect skin.

One of the most exciting things about being a student at the School of American Ballet is dancing in the company's productions, especially *The Nutcracker*, given each year at the Christmas season. When Gelsey was ten, she played an angel. Every year after that she found her name listed among the students chosen for a role.

Dancing in a performance was different from dancing in class. A full orchestra played the music instead of a single piano. The stars of the New York City Ballet danced the leading roles. When the curtain swept open, the huge theater seemed like a dark cave alive with people. It was scary, but fun and exciting, too.

Gelsey progressed rapidly in classes at the school. She began to work on her toes for about five minutes at the end of each class, and finally, she took a class on toe. She moved into advanced classes with Stanley Williams and with Mr. B himself.

She was developing into a fast dancer, with clean, sharp movements, exactly the qualities that Balanchine needed for his pure dance ballets. He noticed dancers who had them, and in time he would notice Gelsey.

"You cared more than anything in the world how you impressed him," Gelsey remembers.

Her years of being a student ended at fifteen when she was invited to join the New York City Ballet. Becoming a professional, however, did not mean the end of classes. Gelsey still had to work on turnout and loosening her muscles. "I can never skip classes the way some dancers can," she says.

After she joined the company, Gelsey ran to the list of performers each time it was posted for a new ballet. But she never found her name there. She swallowed her disappointment and went on to class. The spring season wore on. "I just watched and it was very frustrating, I got angry and impatient."

Summer came, and finally, when the company was at its summer home at Saratoga Springs, New York, Gelsey found her name listed for *Symphony in C*. She took her place in the ensemble as the youngest company member. After that assignment, Gelsey found herself regularly in the ensemble. She was learning more and more of the ballets in the company's repertory, and she loved every minute.

If anything flawed Gelsey's early years with the New York City Ballet, it was competing with Johnna, who was already with the company when Gelsey joined it. "Why can't you be adagio like your sister?" Mr. B would ask, referring to Johnna's smooth motions that flowed into each other. To Johnna he'd say, "Go home and learn to jump like Gelsey." One of their friends, John Clifford, remembers seeing both sisters crying in the wings when the other performed well. Jealousy bothered both girls.

When they were both chosen for leading roles in *Reveries,* Gelsey was worried. The comparison would be so obvious. But it turned out better than Gelsey expected. Each role was fashioned to the sisters' unique styles. "We're lucky we're so different," Gelsey said with relief.

Christmas approached, and with it, *The Nutcracker.* Sixteen-year-old Gelsey danced the leading role of the Sugar Plum Fairy. No one so young had ever been chosen to dance the lead before. It had always gone to one of the experienced soloists. Young Gelsey made up for her age with hard work. "She took the ballet by right, as a young princess," wrote Clive Barnes of her beautiful performance.

Recognition came in more than words. The company promoted the young dancer to the rank of soloist. Her salary rose from $130 to $200 weekly. Even more important than the promotion or raise was being chosen to dance the lead in a new ballet. Mr. B picked her for

Gelsey as the Firebird *in Balanchine's spectacular 1970 produc-tion.*

the title role in his new production of *The Firebird*. He choreographed the ballet to fit Gelsey's talents.

Everything about the ballet was completely new. Sets were designed with brilliant swirls of color by the famous artist Marc Chagall. Gelsey had costume fittings with Madame Karinska over and over again until the golden plumed costume was exactly right.

On opening night Gelsey waited nervously in the wings. She scraped her toe shoes in the rosin box, and let Johnna touch her throat for luck. Then, gliding swiftly in her gold plumage, she flew onstage at the New York State Theater. It was May 28, 1970. "She lit up the stage like a fiery Tinkerbell," one critic wrote. *The Firebird* had made a star of Gelsey at seventeen.

Now she attracted attention outside of the ballet world. A long interview appeared in *Seventeen* magazine, and *Life* gave her a big picture spread. She spoke openly and freely about her career and about her relationship with her mother. Gelsey was proud of Mrs. Kirkland's job as special projects director at *Sports Illustrated*. And she boasted about her mother's riding to work on a bicycle through heavy New York traffic. Gelsey lived alone with her mother now. Jack Kirkland had died of a heart ailment in 1969 and never lived to see Gelsey's stardom on the ballet stage.

But she was secretive about her private life. "I'm a dancer," she said in the *Seventeen* interview. "The rest I'd rather keep to myself. If I couldn't dance, I don't know what I would do with myself."

Over the next two years, Gelsey never had to worry about what to do with herself because she danced nearly all the time. The New York City Ballet had some of its busiest seasons, and Gelsey carried her share of the load. She had become the perfect Balanchine dancer.

Gelsey at seventeen with her dog, Westminster.

Her movements were as quick, clean, and precise as the cut edges of a diamond.

In 1972, Gelsey was promoted to principal dancer, and she worked even harder. The company ended the spring season with a Stravinsky Festival. They danced both old and new ballets to almost everything that the composer had written. Instead of the usual two or three new works, twenty new dances premiered.

During the week-long festival, the dancers were exhausted. Between numbers they usually sat on property tables set up outside the dressing rooms. They talked to each other or knitted leg warmers. During the Stravinsky Festival, they slumped against the wall, saving every bit of energy for appearances onstage.

The company repeated the Stravinsky ballets in Saratoga Springs that summer. Seven thousand people crowded the enormous outdoor theater. The summer ended with an appearance at the Olympics in Munich. The New York Ballet appeared as the cultural representative of the United States. No sooner had they returned to New York than they had to reboard charter jets for a tour of the Soviet Union. One hundred company members, five thousand ballet slippers and costumes, sixty thousand pounds of scenery, and the company's own linoleum floor traveled to Russia.

Any dancer feels a special excitement about a tour to Russia, at one time the center of the ballet world. Balanchine and many of the dancers and choreographers of his generation started ballet training there.

For Gelsey the tour proved especially important. In Leningrad she watched a class, rehearsal, and performance at the Kirov, Mikhail Baryshnikov's home company. While she was there, she met him and shook hands. When the New York City Ballet performed, Gelsey took the lead in *Theme and Variations,* a beautiful but difficult ballroom ballet. She had danced very poorly, she thought, and she was embarrassed when she learned that Baryshnikov had been in the audience.

He had a different opinion. "What amazed us in Leningrad was that she was not headlined more," he said later. He was so impressed that two years later, she was the one he chose to become his partner.

Not headlining a single dancer is a policy of the New York City Ballet. Its reputation rests on the ability of the entire company to perform the Balanchine ballets to perfection. Instead of relying on a single important role, Balanchine stresses the look of the whole ballet—his own brand of pure ballet with classic steps set to music. "A star is a personality," says Balanchine. "I don't want personalities, I want dancers." Perhaps it is Balanchine himself who is the star of the company.

While 1972 brought triumphs for Gelsey, Johnna grew more and more discouraged and left the New York City Ballet. She said, "Mr. B expected the same from both of us, even though we have very different techniques and personalities. We don't even look alike." It was Johnna now who suffered from comparisons.

Later Johnna joined the smaller Los Angeles Ballet, where John Clifford worked as choreographer and director. "I excel more here," Johnna explained. "John challenges me to do better."

After the Russian tour, the New York City Ballet opened its fall season. By now, Gelsey had learned almost all of the roles in the company's repertory, and she turned with ease from one ballet to another. But she was growing restless. An ambitious dancer, she felt that she ought to learn some of the great fairy-tale ballet roles. When she tried to learn some, she found that she

The Kirkland sisters dancing in Reveries, *a New York City Ballet production.*

could not do the new roles while keeping up with Balanchine's difficult ballets.

And then, suddenly, she had more serious worries. Midway through the spring 1973 season, she injured her foot. It was an injury that all dancers dread, and she could not dance at all. She could not finish the spring season and had to sit out the summer.

Injuries swept over the company like measles that year. Although dance is not usually considered as hazardous as football, the strains are similar to those in contact sports. Coming out of a leap, a dancer may turn an ankle, and some dancers feel terror each time they take to the air. The tiniest flaw on the stage or rehearsal room floor may cause a slip. Injuries for both dancers and athletes have the same results—physical activity must stop until the strained muscles and tendons are healed.

Gelsey had had problems before. After learning the almost impossible lead in *Theme and Variations,* she suffered from tendonitis, a swelling of the tendons of the leg that causes severe pain. Now she had to change her technique in order to save her career. She felt that she had to go ahead on her own, and to her this meant dropping Balanchine's classes even though the other dancers resented it. "I had to do it on my own," Gelsey has said, "without anybody's approval and with everybody's disapproval."

It turned out that not quite everyone disapproved. Mr. B respected her decision, and after her recovery, he continued to give her the roles she danced so well. During the spring season of 1974, Gelsey was a jewel. Her role was that of a ruby, in fact, in Balanchine's *Jewels.* Taken with the dazzling display of gems in Tiffany's Fifth Avenue shop window, Mr. B had built a ballet on the beauty of rubies, emeralds, and diamonds.

This was the important spring of 1974, the spring when Baryshnikov defected in Toronto.

Like Gelsey he had danced since childhood. Born in Riga, Latvia, of Russian parents, he was chosen to train with the Kirov Ballet in Leningrad. In Russia it is a great honor for boys and girls to be selected for the Kirov. Parents gladly send their children, although they have to leave home and live in Leningrad.

Mikhail was a star student in spite of the fact that he didn't seem to take himself seriously. He often joked and came to class in torn red tights and a wildly flowered shirt. He teased. He mimicked. His approach to dance was more carefree than Gelsey's, and yet his strength of purpose was as great as hers. He became a leading dancer at the Kirov and made famous the roles created for him there.

What is so unusual about Baryshikov's dancing? "His daring leaps. He seems more at home in the air than on the ground," writes Hubert Saal in *Newsweek*. Others say that his lungs are filled with helium, so long does he seem to stay in the air.

During their first season, Gelsey found his humor catching. She even picked up a bit of his carefree approach to dance. She began to call him "Misha," his Russian nickname. When a romance flared between them, their fans were delighted. Gelsey would not talk about it in public, however. If asked about her co-star, she would smile and say only, "Misha is a very charming boy."

Before long she had the chance to study a famous character in ballet—Giselle.

If actors love to play Hamlet, ballet dancers long to be Giselle. The story is based on a German folk tale

Gelsey and Mikhail Baryshnikov as fairy-tale sweethearts in Giselle.

about a young peasant woman who dies for the love of a duke. The role is one of the most difficult in ballet. It requires acting skill to portray the passionate, grieving Giselle as well as great technique and energy to dance through the full-length ballet.

Gelsey made her debut as Giselle in May 1975 at the Kennedy Center. On all counts, she passed the test with high marks. "It was the coming together of a dancer and a role that had been made for each other . . . . It was the fairy-tale debut little girls dream about," wrote a critic.

Gelsey's confidence grew. "If you really start to believe in . . . the character, then it becomes a part of you," she told Richard Avedon, the famous fashion photographer when he took her picture. "It's not the ballet *Giselle,* it's just—Giselle. It's just not scary anymore."

As Gelsey danced with Misha through 1975 and early 1976, she enchanted audiences in city after city across the country. She had hardly enough time to eat or sleep in between classes, rehearsals, performances, and travel. The hard schedule took its toll.

Other things upset her. The romance with Misha cooled when he became interested in other dancers.

Gelsey injured her foot, and then, during a performance, her entire body began to cramp. Somehow she forced herself to finish the performance, and then she had to leave the tour. Her doctor told her that she was suffering from a potassium deficiency. Gelsey tried to improve her diet, but her weight began to drop and it frightened her.

Even so, she pushed ahead with the summer season—six long weeks at the Metropolitan Opera House in New York. Later she went to Wolf Trap Farm near

Gelsey take a bow with Misha after a dazzling performance of Don Quixote.

Washington, D.C., so thin that she appeared as wispy as the wood nymphs she portrayed. But weak as she was, her strengths as a dancer carried her through a performance of the *Don Quixote* pas de deux with Misha. The performance was televised, and viewers saw, up close, her very thin, steely strong legs.

Almost immediately, Gelsey was supposed to pack her bags and leave for Hollywood. She and Misha were going to play two young dancers in the movie, *The Turning Point*. It was a wonderful opportunity for both of them. Yet Gelsey had already gone beyond her strength, and she knew she couldn't keep up. She had to have time to rest and gain some weight. She announced that she was dropping out. Her role went to Leslie Browne. "It was frightening to feel myself changing and perhaps losing what I had," she later told John Gruen of the *New York Times*.

If she lost what she had, what would she do? That thought must have nagged at her constantly. She, the dancer who said, "I don't know what I'd do if I couldn't dance."

In low spirits and poor health, she retreated to Scottsdale, Arizona, to rest. Desert sun, a healthy diet, and exercise began to restore her body. Johnna visited Gelsey and reported, "She's fine now. She just needs to build up her strength."

And build it up she did, enough to rejoin the American Ballet Theatre in late 1976. She did not take on a full schedule at once, but she appeared in *Giselle* and danced in a benefit.

When it was time to begin getting ready for the spring season, she was rehearsing old roles, learning new ones, and dancing in as fine a form as ever. Gelsey being Gelsey, she took on another nearly impossible challenge. She started to learn the role that may well be the most difficult in ballet. It was the Odette-Odile lead in *Swan Lake,* perhaps the most famous ballet of all time. Odette-Odile is an enchanted swan, sometimes white and good and sometimes black and seductive. They are both danced by the same person.

Tickets were sold out weeks before the performance. Some people were frankly more interested in seeing if fragile Gelsey could get through the role than they were in seeing *Swan Lake.*

John Gruen observed a rehearsal for the *New York Times* and noted her patient approach. She worked out the role slowly from beginning to end, striving for perfection each step of the way. Sometimes even her patience gave way. "I can't do it. It's not right. That was awful!" she would complain from time to time. Then she would make Ivan Nagy, her partner, go through each "awful" sequence until she was satisfied with it.

On June 10, 1977, she stepped into the white costume and danced onstage. Incredibly, she added challenges to the already difficult role. Instead of pirouetting once, she tried it three times. She held balances unbelievably long. Then she dressed as the black Odile and danced flawlessly through the famous solo with whipping *fouettes*. At the last note of music, the people in the audience rose to their feet and greeted her with cheers. Her fans went wild.

Swan Lake was a sign of better and better things to come. In July 1977, Gelsey went on to dance for Queen Elizabeth during the silver jubilee celebration in London. Then she and her company went on to a European tour.

Back in her own country in the spring of 1978, she danced for President and Mrs. Carter when they attended the premiere of Baryshnikov's full-length *Don Quixote* at Kennedy Center. Once again Baryshnikov had picked Gelsey as his partner. She danced the role of Kitri in a ballet that required her to perform a dramatic role with the speed and precision of her New York City Ballet days. It was a perfect blending of her talents.

Her appearance in *Don Quixote* also earned her a cover story in *Time* magazine, an honor reserved only for top-flight newsmakers. Gelsey, it seems, had made news for ballet. On the May 1, 1978, issue, she streaks across *Time's* cover in a brilliant pink dress, with her legs turned out in an unbelievable extension.

A short time later she was interviewed on television after a performance of *Theme and Variations,* danced with Baryshnikov.

"How did it feel to become a national celebrity?" the announcer asked.

Gelsey, relaxed and happy, backstage during rehearsal.

She ran her tongue around the inside of her mouth, which was no doubt dry as a bone from the difficult dance. "It changed my life," she paused, smiling, "for about five minutes. Then I went on with what I am always doing." It takes only one guess to know what that is—exercises at the barre, rehearsals, and performances.

But Gelsey has changed. After her illness, she began to see a psychiatrist in New York. She has relaxed more. Dancers notice that she is easier to work with now that she is not so demanding of herself and others.

At the end of the 1978 spring season, Baryshnikov announced that he was leaving the American Ballet Theatre for the New York City Ballet. The pas de deux between them has ended. Now they are each off on their own solos, and like Misha, Gelsey has become a superstar.

"U.S. Ballet Soars," read the cover title of *Time* when her photograph appeared. Young Gelsey is soaring ahead of the rest.

Other
Outstanding Women

In addition to the five women featured in this book, there are many hundreds more who have contributed greatly to the dance. Although it is impossible to discuss them all, here are a few more of America's foremost dancers.

LUCIA CHASE (1907-   ). Dancer, director, patron, and founder, Lucia Chase has been all of these and more. Born into a wealthy family, Chase studied drama, voice, and dance during her early years. In 1940, she and Richard Pleasant, manager of the Mordkin Ballet, founded the American Ballet Theatre. They wanted not only to create a company of American dancers, but also to bring in many choreographers, allowing them to supervise their own work. Chase backed the company financially and appeared as its principal dancer. In 1945 she became co-director with Oliver Smith. Through the years she has stayed with the American Ballet Theatre, contributing much of her wealth and all of her time and energy. Today, along with the New York City Ballet, the American Ballet Theatre leads the ranks of American companies.

FRANCESCA CORKLE (1952-   ). A dancer with a flare for drama and a personality that beams through her performances, Francesca Corkle is ideally suited to the Joffrey Company. Leaning to the modern and offbeat, it calls upon many forms of dance and theater to present ballet that ranges from the traditional to the most contemporary. Corkle has been with the Joffrey Company since she joined it in 1967, when she was fifteen. Although Joffrey gives no star billing, Corkle has received the critical attention and praise worthy of a star. In 1976 she charmed a vast television audience as she floated dreamily through Robert Joffrey's romantic ballet, *Remembrances,* one of the "Dance in America" series.

KATHERINE DUNHAM (1910-   ). Katherine Dunham's career as a dancer, choreographer, and teacher has been long and influential. It was she who focused attention on the black dancer as a performing artist. During the 1930s and 1940s, the Katherine Dunham Dance Group, an all-black company, performed dances rooted deep in the culture of black people. She also used contemporary themes with the aim of showing the black experience today through dance. She is a respected scholar, who still works tirelessly to further the cause of ethnic dance. She directs the Performing Arts Training Center at Southern Illinois University and teaches elsewhere as a visiting professor.

CYNTHIA GREGORY (1946-   ). Cynthia Gregory demonstrated unusual talent as soon as she started her professional career with the Santa Monica Civic Ballet. Then, like climbing a pyramid, she went from dance company to dance company until she joined the American Ballet Theatre at nineteen. It took her only two years to become a principal dancer there. "Stunning, smooth as silk, superb," write critics of her solos. Guest performances have earned her a worldwide reputation, and Rudolf Nureyev has choreographed a new full-length version of *Raymonda* just for her.

JUDITH JAMISON (1944-   ). Judith Jamison might be called the superstar of modern dance. She dances splendidly, and she seems larger than life on stage. After training in ballet at the Philadelphia Dance Academy and in modern dance at Joan Kerr's Dance School, she joined the Ailey Company in 1965. There she has remained to build a spectacular career. In 1971 Jamison reached stardom with *Cry,* one of the longest and most demanding solos ever choreographed. It was a dance that Alvin Ailey created for her and dedicated to "all black women, especially our mothers." In 1976 she reached new heights when she performed with Mikhail Baryshnikov in a million-dollar dance festival put on by the company to honor Duke Ellington. Her own words best sum up her life as a dancer. "I am a dancer who happens to be black. . . . I have always tried to learn not only *how* to dance, but what it is for *me* to dance."

SHIRLEY MACLAINE (1934-   ). In 1954, Shirley MacLaine went to Hollywood to star in her first movie with what she later came to see as the best training ever—fifteen years as a dancer, mainly in ballet. She had come from *Pajama Game,* then a smash hit on Broadway. As understudy to Carol Haney, she had danced and sung her way through the starring role for a month while Haney nursed a broken leg. Fifteen years as one of Hollywood's leading ladies in both musicals and dramas followed. Then, after putting all her energies into Senator George McGovern's unsuccessful bid for the presidency in 1972, she reached a low point in her life. It was time for a change. She organized a group of American women for a visit to China, and when she came home, returned to the stage in a musical revue, *A Gypsy in My Soul.* After an international tour, in which she was compared to such entertainers as Danny Kaye and Ethel Merman, she starred in *The Turning Point,* a movie about the dreams and disappointments of ballet. Actress, author of two books, and a person uncommonly aware of the problems of our time, Shirley MacLaine is a woman who left dance to enrich our lives and her own.

JULIET PROWSE (1937-   ). Long, beautiful legs are an asset to any dancer, and Juliet Prowse uses hers in dazzling kicks, splits, and high steps. A star of Hollywood and Las Vegas, she was born in South Africa and came to this country in 1958. The following year she captured a leading role in the movie version of *Can-Can.* This led to starring roles in other movies, but lavish, slick nightclub reviews are her most recent domain. Her fast-paced show usually starts with a medley of short dance numbers, leading to spectacular finale, such as a ballet set to Ravel's *Bolero.* Prowse dances with an ever-increasing intensity, matching the build-up of the music. At the feverish climax, the stage is filled with swirling color and movement. Ballet over, silence and arrested motion freeze the room. Then the audience explodes in applause, cheers, and whistles to thank her for bringing them such fantasy and delight.

RUTH ST. DENIS (1878-1968). This dancer, who changed the course of American dance history, turned to the Orient for inspiration. Dancing in exotic, flowing costumes of India and Egypt, she brought a romantic world to many people that they had never seen before. She was a tall, beautiful woman, whose body and arm movements flowed as freely and smoothly as the gowns she wore. Together with her husband and dancing partner, Ted Shawn, she founded the Denishawn School. It was a school that influenced an entire generation of dancers, including Martha Graham, Doris Humphrey, and Charles Weidman. Her freedom of movement and different themes opened the eyes of those in dance to new possibilities.

MARIA TALLCHIEF (1925-   ). The first U.S. *prima ballerina,* or "dancer of the first rank," is the grand-daughter of an Osage Indian. Maria Tallchief began studying ballet seriously at the age of eight when her family moved from Oklahoma to Los Angeles, mainly to help their two musically talented daughters. She first danced professionally with the Ballet Russe and in 1947 joined the Ballet Society, which had just been established by George Balanchine. This new company would later become known as the world-famous New York City Ballet. Tallchief and Balanchine had a close artistic association which both led up to and followed their marriage and annulment. A tireless worker and a dancer of rare talent, Tallchief became an American ambassador of dance to the ballet centers of Europe. She retired in 1966, but to anyone lucky enough to have seen her dance, her performances as the Firebird, the Swan Queen, and Miss Julie live on as legends. See *Maria Tallchief: The Story of an American Indian* by Marion E. Gridley for the full story of her life.

Suggested Reading

de Mille, Agnes. *Dance to the Piper*. Little, Brown & Co., 1952. *And Promenade Home*. Little, Brown & Co., 1958.
  Two lively witty books that describe a choreographer's life in her own words.
Duncan, Isadora. *My Life*. Livewright, 1927.
  A great dancer tells her own dramatic story.
Gridley, Marion E. *Maria Tallchief: The Story of an American Indian*. Dillon Press, 1973.
  Written especially for young readers, this biography sheds light on the dancer's Osage heritage.
Gruen, John. *The Private World of Ballet*. Viking Press, 1975.
  Based on personal interviews, this book looks at the behind-the-scenes life of a dancer.
Krementz, Jill. *A Very Young Dancer*. Knopf, 1976.
  Ten-year-old Stephanie tells us in her own words, with photos by Jill Krementz, what it is like to be a student at the School of American Ballet.
McDonagh, Don. *Complete Guide to Modern Dance*. Doubleday, 1976.
  Everything the interested reader will want to know is found in this guide to modern dance.
Terry, Walter. *The Ballet Companion: A Popular Guide for the Ballet Goer*. Dodd, Mead, & Co., 1968.
  A brief history, definitions of terms, and discussion of style are all included in this easy-to-read book on ballet.

Carol Fowler is a free-lance writer who has contributed both short stories and nonfiction articles to a number of young people's magazines, including *Ingenue, Twelve-Fifteen,* and *Teen Time.* She is the author of *Contributions of Women: Art* and *Daisy Nampeyo: The Story of an American Indian,* also published by Dillon Press.

Ms. Fowler received her B.S. degree from the University of Wisconsin at Madison. After graduation, she taught science at the eighth-grade level for several years. She is currently a member of the California Writer's Club and the American Association of University Women.

She and her husband have three children and live in Walnut Creek, California, where she is a feature writer in the arts for the *Contra Costa Times.*